How To Do Your Own Astrological Chart

-A Beginner's Guide-

ESME MORGAN

ISBN: 149595434X
ISBN-13: 978-1495954344

FOREWORD

Hi, I was a professional astrologer for more than two decades, and having had so many clients express curiosity about how a chart is created and interpreted, I've put together this 'How-To' book on how to do it yourself. It's aimed at beginners who have an interest in astrology but no previous experience in creating a chart.

Astrology is intriguing and fun to work with for so many reasons. To name just a few, astrology can be used to:

- assess a person's character and circumstances

- predict upcoming trends and potential future events

- consider possible influences on work, friends, love, etc

- determine compatibility (or lack of it) between two people

- analyze good and bad influences present on a given day

Contrary to popular belief, you don't have to be a math wizard to do the calculations involved. In this book, you will be instructed on how to either use a computer program to do the calculations for you (highly recommended), or be brave and follow the alternative instructions on how to do it all yourself the hard way.

In the first part of the book, I give you links to where you can download free versions of all the materials you will need, kindly provided for free on various websites. These items comprise:

- a freeware astrology chart calculation computer program

- booklets with info you need for your calculations if you are doing them manually rather than with a computer program, and blank chart forms

The latter part of the book consists of one big reference database in which I've composed individual interpretations for every planet, sign, House and aspect, which you can put together to create a full chart reading.

So, this is not another 'Sun Sign' book, but is about what goes on behind the creating and interpretation of a complete birth chart, and shows you, hopefully easily and painlessly, how to do it yourself. I will try to keep things as simplified and straightforward as possible in order to reduce 'information overload'!

Thanks for looking and I hope you will find this book informative and enjoyable!

CONTENTS

ACKNOWLEDGMENTS

Thank you to all those who bought the original Kindle version of this book. I hope this printed edition will help readers who find a paper adaptation easier to work with than on onscreen one.

PART ONE: CREATING THE CHART

What exactly is an astrological chart, you might well ask? An astrological chart is basically a map of the positions of the planets as they appear in the sky at a given moment for a given location.

The map shows which **sign** each planet was in, which sign was just coming up over the horizon at that moment (that is, the **Rising Sign**, also known as the **Ascendant**), which **House** (12 different specific segments of the chart) each planet was in, and the **aspects** (different degrees of angles) the planets make to each other.

If you're not familiar with any or all of those various different terms, no worries, you'll be learning about them soon in this book.

To get started, obtain the following three bits of info for the chart you want to create:

- **Date of birth**
- **Time of Birth**
- **Place of Birth**

The date of birth must include the correct year (the chart will be wrong if the year is wrong – so, no lying about one's age allowed!), and the time must be as exact as possible for maximum accuracy of the chart.

If it's not possible to find out the exact time, the nearest guess will have to be used. If it is not even possible to guess, then we use 12:00 noon (but it needs to be borne in mind that if we don't have the correct time, then the chart, and therefore its interpretation, will be less accurate).

You then have to find out the coordinates for the place of birth and use them in your calculations, so you also need a geographical atlas that gives latitude and longitude coordinates.

If you don't have such an atlas, you can use a web site that lets you look up these details, for instance LATLONG.net:

http://www.latlong.net/

ASTROLOGY SYMBOLS

First of all, you need to get very well acquainted with the symbols, or glyphs, used in astrology interpretation and what each represents, because you will be working with these symbols all the time. Here they all are summarized with short keyword interpretations.

(Again, these are only keyword descriptions. More in-depth description of what each item means will be given later on in the book.)

The Signs

Aries

Assertive, robust, 'me first', quick-acting, independent

Taurus

Stable, possessive, comfort-loving, down to earth

Ⅱ

Gemini

Communication, travel, intellect, versatility, youthfulness

♋

Cancer

Protective, sensitive, moody, sympathetic, changeable

♌

Leo

Sunny, generous, extrovert, attention-seeking

♍

Virgo

Efficient, organized, precise, eye for detail, science

♎

Libra

Peace-loving, harmony, fairness, love of beauty

Scorpio

Intense, determined, mystery, intrigue, passion

Sagittarius

Straightforward, honest, restless, nonconformist, playful

Capricorn

Ambition, betterment, practical, careful, hard working

Aquarius

Emotionally-detached, inventive, original, eccentricity

Pisces

Sensitive, dreamy, imaginative, empathy, mystical

The Planets

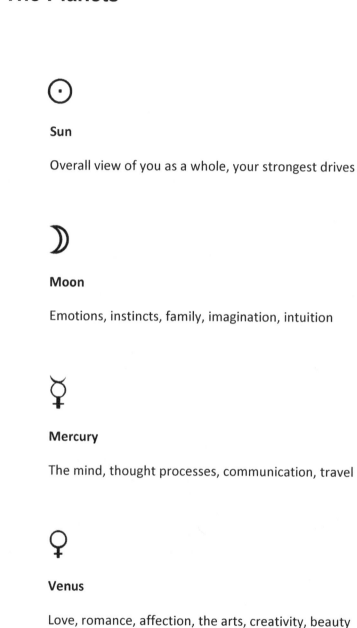

Sun

Overall view of you as a whole, your strongest drives

Moon

Emotions, instincts, family, imagination, intuition

Mercury

The mind, thought processes, communication, travel

Venus

Love, romance, affection, the arts, creativity, beauty

Mars

Drives, ambitions, assertiveness, aggressiveness, power

Jupiter

Expansion, growth, religion, foreign countries, humor

Saturn

Lessons, limitations, serious matters, responsibility

Uranus

Sudden or unexpected things, eccentric, modern

Neptune

Imagination, mystery, intoxication, art, the sea

 or

(glyph varies from country to country)

Pluto

Transformation, new phases, dynamic, hidden

The Aspects

♂

Conjunction (0°)

A strong focal point in the chart

△

Trine (120°)

A strongly fortunate influence

✳

Sextile (60°)

A moderately fortunate influence

☐

Square (90°)

A highly challenging influence

Opposition (180°)

An area of conflict or of a strong give-and-take and/or polarity

Quincunx (150°)

An indication of some minor difficulty or strain

The Houses

An astrological chart is depicted on paper as a large circle divided into 12 pie-slice-shaped segments (we'll take a look at how we depict that, just a few pages from now). These pie-slice segments are referred to as Houses.

Each House represents a different area of a person's life and environment, and these areas are affected according to the meanings of the planets and signs that fall into them.

Below are keyword interpretations of what each House represents:

1

1st House: The ego, one's strongest compulsions, one's appearance

2

2nd House: Money, earnings, spending, possessions

3

3rd House: Communication, short journeys, siblings, early education

4

4th House: Home, domestic environment, family, childhood

5

5th House: Creativity, sports, the arts, love affairs, children

6

6th House: The work environment, health-related matters

7

7th House: Love, marriage, partnerships and other significant relationships

8

8th House: Other people's money, legacies, sex, death,

life's mysteries

9

9th House: Higher education, foreign travel, religion, philosophy

10

10th House: Career, status in the community, how others see you

11

11th House: Friends, social life, group activities, pastimes

12

12th House: The unconscious, dreams, imagination, solitude, spirituality

You now need to do the necessary calculations....

DOING IT THE EASY WAY (Recommended): Using a computer program to do the calculations

This is a much, MUCH easier and more pleasant way than doing the calculations yourself, which is tedious and long-winded. I recommend a nice, simple little freeware program that I've been using for many years called Astrolog, by Walter D. Pullen. Its download address is:

http://www.astrolog.org/astrolog/astfile.htm

On that page, look under "Executables Ready To Run' at the top of the page. Click the first link if you want to download a full Windows installer version, or click the second link if you prefer to download a zipped 'portable' version that you just extract into a folder yourself and that you can copy/move anywhere without having to install it.

Although this program is old, its download page states that it runs on all versions of Windows up to Windows 8, including 64-bit Windows. I can confirm that I run it under all Windows versions up to and including Windows 7, at least the 32-bit versions.

There is a Mac version for download on that page too, but it is not compatible with modern Macs (it doesn't work with either Intel processors or OS X). The best course of action for Mac users is to run the Windows version of Astrolog either with a Windows emulator such as Virtual PC, VirtualBox or Parallels, or by using Bootcamp and booting your Mac into Windows.

As Astrolog is quite an old program, its interface looks old-fashioned, but don't let that put you off. It will do exactly what you need, quickly and simply, to acquire all the info needed to draw a chart, and that's really all that matters in the end. (Plus that it's free.)

And anyway I give you step by step instructions below on how to use it, so don't worry if it looks horrible to you when you start it up.

(Alternatively, if you already know of another chart-calculating program that you prefer, you can of course use that instead.)

But even if you choose to do the work using the astrology software rather than manually, it's worth still reading through the parts of this book that show how to do it manually, just to get a better idea of the processes at work behind the scenes.

HOW TO USE ASTROLOG

INSTALLING THE PROGRAM

- Run the setup file ast54win.exe if you downloaded the installer version, or unzip the zip file ast54win.zip if you downloaded the portable version.

- For the installer version, just leave all the default options as they appear on the installation screen (Figure 1 below), and click Finish.

-

Figure 1: Astrolog Installer screen

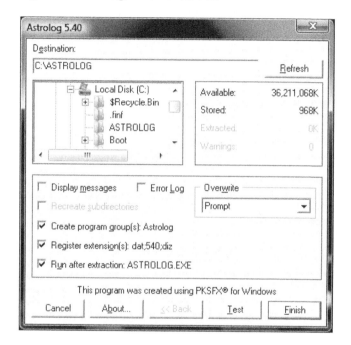

- It will install the program into C:\ASTROLOG (note it doesn't install into Program Files) and will say that the files have been extracted.

- After that, Astrolog will appear in your Windows Start Menu.

NOTE: If you chose to download the portable zipped version instead, then you don't get a shortcut in your Start menu. Instead, inside the folder you extracted, just run the file called ASTROLOG.EXE.

NOTE: If you have any problems getting the installer version to work properly under Windows Vista upwards, where some people can have problems with UAC, administrator rights, and all that rubbish that previous Windows versions didn't inflict on us, then try the portable version instead, which might behave better.

STARTING UP THE PROGRAM FOR THE FIRST TIME

In either case, when you start the program a window will appear that looks like the one in Figure 2 on the next page. It displays a chart of the current date and time, showing all the planetary positions and aspects, and also gives the details in list form in the right hand pane.

This comes up as a fairly small window by default, but you can drag the edges and corners of the window to make it bigger. Clicking the maximize button is not recommended if you have a modern widescreen monitor, as the output was made for old 800x600 resolution monitors and it will make the chart a distorted oval shape. You'll get better results by just dragging and reshaping the window yourself.

In that screen, you can now see what we've been talking about earlier about how the chart looks like a big circle divided into 12 pie-slice shaped segments.

Figure 2: Astrolog main screen (next page). (Note: on your PC screen this will be in multiple pretty colors rather than black and white as reproduced in this book)

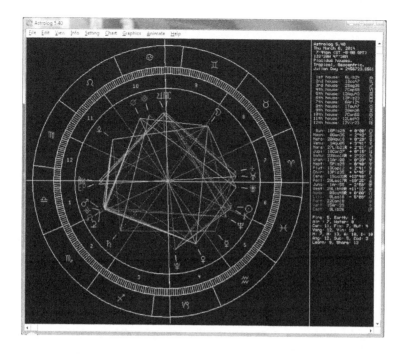

Now, to enter the necessary information on the person for whom you want to do the chart, go into the **Info Menu** and choose **Set Chart Info**.

As illustrated in Figure 3 below, type in:

- Month / Day / Year / Time

- Whether Daylight Savings time or not

- Time Zone

- Longitude / Latitude

- Name

- Location

Enter the info in the same format in which the already-filled-in example information is formatted (see Figure 3 below), and then click **OK**.

Figure 3: Astrolog 'Set Chart Info' box

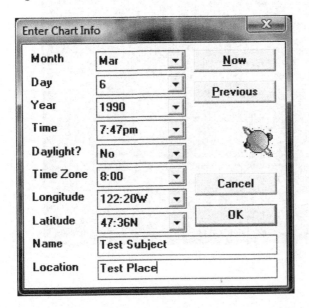

Next, go into the **Setting Menu**. Choose **House System** and then choose **Equal**. (We use the Equal House System in this book for simplicity, but you can investigate other House systems later if you like).

The onscreen chart changes to display the new information you've entered, and so what you now have in front of you is a nice colorful picture of that person's birth chart.

The right hand pane also gives you the Rising Sign, or Ascendant – look to the right of where it says '1st House:' on the pane that is down the right side of the screen.

For example, '1st House: 16Cap52' means that the person's Rising Sign is Capricorn. Capricorn was the sign that was coming up over the horizon at the moment of birth, and 16 degrees 52 seconds was how far into the sign of Capricorn the horizon was at that moment.

Underneath the listing of the House cusps, the list then goes on to give the sign and degree of each planet. (A few asteroids as well, which is beyond the scope of this book but you can always learn about these at a later time – they're not normally used in regular astrology but are sometimes looked at as an extra influence on a chart.)

What it means:

- **'1st House: 16Cap52'** means, as we've just discussed, that the Ascendant is 16º 52' Capricorn

- **'Sun: 26Vir08'** means the Sun is in 26º 08' Virgo

- **'Moon 18ºAri17'** means the Moon is in 18º 17' Aries

And so on. Note that the Midheaven doesn't appear in the lists, you need to look at the onscreen chart itself to find it. Look for '**MC**' near the top of the chart.

MC is used as the standard abbreviation for Midheaven (it stands for Medium Coeli, Latin for 'middle of the sky').

ONWARD!

If you used a computer application to do the calculations for you, you can now skip to 'Drawing the Chart' in the next section.

You are now armed with all the info you need to draw and interpret the chart: the planets' signs and degrees, and the Ascendant and Midheaven signs and degrees.

Otherwise, if you prefer to do it all manually yourself, carry on from the next page:

CONSTRUCTING THE CHART: DOING IT THE HARD WAY

(If you're using Astrolog or other computer app to do the calculations, skip this section and proceed ahead to 'Drawing the Chart'.)

For those who want to be hardcore and do the math rather than using a computer program, before you get started you will first need two booklets:

- A **Table of Houses** for the part of the world that you (or whoever you're doing the chart for) live in.

- An **Ephemeris** for the year you will be working with (these are also available for groups of years).

Try to use an Ephemeris that shows the planets' positions at noon – this is the most common type and is what we'll be using in our exercises in this book.

These booklets may be found in astrology and/or occult bookshops. But if you have trouble finding them, here are alternatives, and they're free:

FREE DOWNLOADABLE EPHEMERIS

Very helpfully, a free downloadable ephemeris can be found on Astro.com:

http://www.astro.com/swisseph/swepha_e.htm

This is split up into individual years, each of which are in pdf format and can be downloaded and read with Acrobat Reader, Foxit Reader, or other PDF reader of your choice. Just click on the year of your (or whomever's) birth within the first area on that page, and download the file.

FREE DOWNLOADABLE TABLE OF HOUSES

Unfortunately it seems to be difficult to find these online for free. The best I could find after quite a bit of searching is only for Northern latitudes of 22 to 56 degrees. It can be downloaded, in various formats including PDF and Kindle, from Internet Archive:

http://archive.org/details/sphericalbasisof00dalt

Really, all things considered, I strongly recommend using Astrolog or other chart calculation computer software of your choice instead. But if you're determined to take the pen and paper approach and you've found a suitable Table of Houses for your location, read on:

A straightforward example chart

Again, this part only needs to be worked through by those who are NOT using Astrolog or another computer app but are doing the calculations manually. But those who have used Astrolog or similar may still find it interesting to read in order to get the full behind-the-scenes info on the technicalities involved in chart calculation.

We have someone who can give us an exact time of

birth, and they were born in London at 0º longitude, so this is about as straightforward as you get. Any other longitude requires an extra calculation, which we'll cover later in this section.

The birth data are as follows:

- Date of birth: 7 April 1982

- Time of birth: 8:20 a.m.

- Place of birth: London

Latitude and Longitude

The first thing we need to do is determine the latitude and longitude of the person's birthplace. Any good atlas that shows these coordinates can be used.

London has a latitude of 51º 32' North, and a longitude of 0º.

NOTE: Summer Time / Daylight Savings Time:

The birth time in this case is in British Summer Time (Daylight Savings Time). The time of birth has to be adjusted to Standard Time before we can work with it, though. This is easily accomplished by just subtracting one hour.

So, the time used for our calculations will now be 7:20 a.m. GMT.

Do the math!

Opening the ephemeris to the page that contains the date and time in question, we find something like this under April:

```
Date   Sidereal Time    Sun Long    Moon Long
       Hr Min Sec
7      01  01  44        17° 20'     6°  16'
```

Some ephemeris books give more information than this, but we are only concerned with the Sidereal Time and the longitudes (positions) of the planets ('Sun Long', 'Moon Long', etc.).

(Sidereal Time is, basically, an astronomical time scale that is based on the Earth's rate of rotation measured relative to the fixed stars.)

Calculate the amount of time from birth time to noon:

- 12:00 noon

- -7:20 a.m.

- =4:40 hours from birth time to noon

This difference between noon and the birth time is called the Interval.

Next subtract the interval from the Sidereal Time:

- 01:01.44

- -4:40.00

Oh, hang on, in this particular case, the resultant Sidereal time will be a smaller figure than the interval, so that it's a minus figure. But it's not a problem. When this happens, simply add 24 hours to the Sidereal Time. So, now our calculation looks as follows:

- 25:01.44

- -4:40.44

- =20:21.44

Now comes an adjustment called the Acceleration On The Interval. This is done to account for the difference between Sidereal Time and 'Earth' time. It's calculated at ten seconds per hour.

So it's 40 seconds for four hours, and we can estimate another 7 seconds for the extra 40 minutes. Our acceleration works out to 47 seconds, and we subtract that from our last figure:

- 20:21.44

- -.47

- =20:20.57

The figure of 20:20.57 is what we're after – that gives us what the Sidereal Time at Greenwich was at the time of the subject's birth. This is now what we work with as the person's time of birth.

That's almost it for the calculations - we have one more to do later, to adjust the position of the Moon to its exact place at the time of birth (because the position of the Moon moves much more quickly relative to the Earth than those of the planets do).

Here's a review of what we've done so far:

- 12:00 (noon)

- -7:20 a.m. (birth time)

- =4:40 (interval)

Then,

- 01:01.44 (Sidereal Time)

- -4:40.00 (interval)

- =20:21.44

So,

- 20:21.44

- -.47 (acceleration on interval)

- =20:20.57 (Sidereal GMT at time of birth)

You can follow that example for any birth occurring in London (or anywhere else in the Northern Hemisphere that is at 0º longitude).

Births occurring after noon

Instead of finding the interval to noon from the birth time, you need to find the interval from noon to the birth time.

For example, if someone was born at 4:00 p.m., you calculate the hours from noon to 4:00 p.m. Therefore, 4 hours is the interval. And in these cases, the acceleration is added rather than subtracted.

The Table of Houses

It's now time to discover our example person's Ascendant (Rising Sign, the sign just coming up over the horizon at the moment of birth) and Midheaven (the sign directly overhead at the time of birth).

Open the Table of Houses to either the page headed 'London' if it has one, or else to a page on which you can find figures for London's latitude, 51º 32' North.

You'll see something like this:

```
Sidereal time    10  11  12  Asc
```

as the headings over a series of columns that show the Sidereal Time ranging from 00:00.00 to 24:00.00.

For our example, we want to find 20:20.57, so look down the Sidereal Time column until you find the nearest to 20:20.57. My Table of Houses shows the following:

Sidereal Time	10	11	12	Asc
	Aqu	Aqu	Tau	Gem
H. M. S.				
20 17 03	2°	27°	7°	5° 32
20 21 11	3°	28°	9°	6° 53
20 25 19	4°	29°	11°	8° 12

The nearest listed time to 20:20.57 is 20:21.11, so that's the time we start from to find the Ascendant. As the time listed is a bit greater than the time we are dealing with, bring the figure of 6º 53' down a bit to compensate for the difference. In this case, we are going to just round it off to the nearest whole number, 6º. So, our Ascendant is 6º Gemini, give or take a few seconds.

NOTE: You can calculate a closer figure that includes seconds if you want to be as accurate as possible, but because this book is aimed at beginners we are going to use rounding-off for the sake of simplicity.

The only other figure we're concerned with here is the one under the heading '10'; this figure gives the Midheaven and the degree it falls at.

In this case, we can see that the Midheaven, under the heading of '10', is 3º Aquarius.

The other headings (11, 12, 2, 3) are for using other methods of House division than the Equal House system which is used in this book. I find the Equal House system works the best for me, but you can go on to learn about other systems and decide on your own preferences.

Astrolog users pick up again from here!

DRAWING THE CHART

You can download ready-printed blank chart forms for free from various places in the web. For example, there's a nice free selection here for personal use:

www.internationalastrologers.com/blank chart pg 3.htm

Or, you can use this Google Image search to look for others:

https://www.google.co.uk/search?q=blank+astrology+chart+free

If you prefer to hand draw everything yourself rather than using a readymade form, then on the top half of a large piece of paper (A4 or long letter is a good size), inscribe a generous-sized circle using a compass. (Or draw it freehand if you're accurate at drawing nice circles!)

Divide it into twelve equal portions, number the portions from one to twelve, and then draw another, bigger, circle around the first circle. The finished item should have a sort of wagon wheel look to it, as in Figure 6 next page. (The small 'hub'-like circle in the middle is optional, but I like to put it in. It gives you a nice little area in which to write the person's name, or add a design or some other embellishment.)

Figure 6

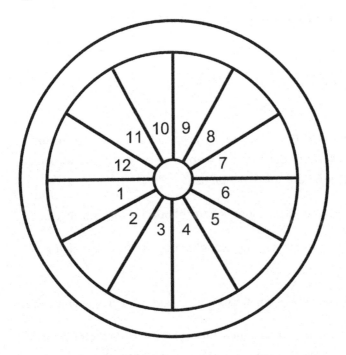

The horizontal line across the circle represents the horizon. The part of the chart that represents the Ascendant or Rising Sign is the left end of the horizontal line. The left end of that line also represents the beginning of the first House, as depicted by the number 1 just below that line.

The twelve astrological signs go into the outer circle starting at the first House, the pie-slice shaped segment numbered '1', as in Figure 7 next page. The first sign to be entered onto the chart form will be the Rising Sign, and then we fill in the other signs in their sequential order.

Figure 7

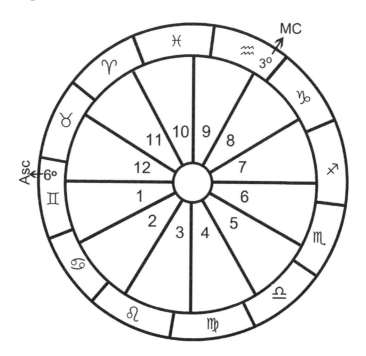

In Figure 7, we've written in the degree of the Rising Sign along with the symbol for the sign (so, 6º Gemini in this example), which gives us our 1st House cusp.

Each numbered pie-slice segment is called a House, and each House represents 30º of the complete 360º circle.

In Figure 7 you can see how the signs have now been written in around the circle, in sequence starting from Gemini, and how the Ascendant (Asc) and Midheaven (MC) have been notated by showing their degrees plus little arrows to draw attention to their positions.

Each sign takes up 30º of the circle, just as the Houses do.

Note that unless the Ascendant is at exactly 0º of a sign, the dividing lines between the signs will not match up with the dividing lines between the Houses. Those will follow their own different set of dividing lines, which are determined by the degree of the Ascendant. So in this case, 6º Gemini means that each House will start at 6º of each subsequent sign, rather than its default of 0º.

The lines that divide the signs and also the lines that divide the Houses are called **cusps**. When a planet is referred to as 'on the cusp' of some sign or House, we mean that the planet falls on or very near one of these dividing lines.

So, we've drawn 12 cusps in the outer ring of the chart to demarcate each 30 degree span of each of the 12 signs.

In our sample chart the Ascendant is at 6º, so each House starts at 6º of its respective sign: the first House starts at 6º Gemini, the second House starts at 6º Cancer, the third at 6º Leo, and so on until we come full circle to Taurus on the 12th House cusp.

Okay, so now you are going to fill in your own chart with the details you either got from Astrolog, or for those who are doing it themselves, the details you will get from the Ephemeris as described below.

BACK TO THE EMPHEMERIS

For non-Astrolog users:

In the ephemeris, go to the date in question (in our example, 7 April 1982) and look at the longitudes of the planets for that day. These figures show exactly where each planet goes in our chart.

Enter the symbols, or glyphs, for the planets at the relevant places around the chart (except for the Moon, which we will deal with in a minute), accompanied by the figure in degrees shown for each planet.

For instance, in the case of our example person, the Sun's longitude is given as 17º 20' Aries. Write in the glyph for the Sun followed by the degree, as in Figure 8 below in which the completed chart is shown with all planets and their longitudes filled in.

NOTE: For the purpose of this beginners-level book, I round off all figures to their nearest whole degree numbers just to make things simpler. But you can include the exact seconds if you prefer to do so.

Now do the same for all the other planets except for the Moon, which we will deal with in the next paragraph. For Mercury onwards, jot down the longitude shown in the ephemeris for each of the remaining planets, and then write their glyph and degree on the chart just the way it's been done in Figure 8 for our example chart.

For Astrolog users:

Just copy all the necessary information displayed on your Astrolog chart screen to a blank chart form as depicted in Figure 8 on the next page.

Figure 8

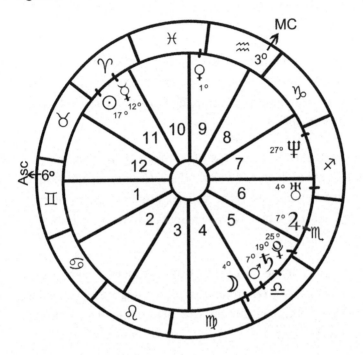

Calculating the Moon's position*

*Again, this is only for those who are NOT using Astrolog or similar application, which will have done this calculation for you. If using Astrolog, skip ahead to the next section, 'The Aspects'.

When dealing with an a.m. birth, we look at the Moon's position at noon the day in question, and its position on the previous day (for p.m. births, it's the day in question and the following day).

In our example case, we find that on 6th April, the Moon's position at noon was 23º 10' Virgo. On 7th April, the Moon's position at noon was 6º 16' Libra.

We need to find the difference between the noon positions of the Moon for the two dates. Remember that each sign takes up 30º, so it's approximately 7º of Virgo plus approximately 6º of Libra. So this adds up to approximately 13º that the Moon moved in the 24-hour period between 6th April and 7th April .

Or in other words, the Moon moves just a little over half a degree per hour.

As our example interval between the birth time and noon is 4 hours and 40 minutes (or 4 2/3 hours) we need to just do some quick multiplying:

- 4 (hours) x ½ (degree of Moon's movement) = 2º

- 40 (mins) x ½ (degree of Moon's movement)= 20'

If we now subtract these 2º 20' from April 7th's noon Moon position of 6º 16', we end up with a rounded-off figure of 4º.

(Again, you can calculate a more precise figure to the nearest second if you want greater accuracy, but in this book we're rounding things off for the sake of simplicity.)

And this is our adjusted figure for the Moon at the time of birth, which we can now fill in the glyph and degree for on our chart form the same way we did for the other planets.

The Aspects

Next we write up and interpret all of the aspects that occur in the person's chart. Aspects are degree angles that planets make to each other, and they carry meanings that are just as important as those of the planets, signs and Houses.

Aspects add either stressful or fortunate influences to the various spheres of life, as will be explained in more detail in the next section.

The aspects are as follows::

- Conjunction: two planets 0º apart (8º orb)

- Sextile: two planets 60º apart (5º orb)

- Square: two planets 90º apart (8º orb)

- Trine: two planets 120º apart (8º orb)

- Quincunx: two planets 150º apart (2º orb)

- Opposition: two planets 180º apart (8º orb)

What is meant by '**orb**' is the number of degrees of tolerance that can be allowed when determining whether two planets aspect each other or not.

For instance, in our sample chart there is a 182º opposition between the Sun (17º Aries) and Saturn (19º Libra). The exact figure of 180º for an opposition is off by only 2º, so this is well within the required orb of 8º.

But if the Sun had been, for example, 6º Aries, the difference between it and Saturn would have been 167º which would have been 13º away from 180º, and as 13º falls outside of the orb of 8º, it is not close enough to be an opposition.

The Aspect Grid

This is a table of rows and columns which you fill in with glyphs representing each of the aspects that the planets, Ascendant and Midheaven make to each other.

It gives us a nice organized graphical method of seeing all the aspects at a glance, to make interpreting the chart quicker and easier. It looks sort of like a table in a word processing document, or a simple spreadsheet from a spreadsheet program.

Following on from having drawn your chart on the upper half of your sheet of paper, now draw an empty aspect grid onto the bottom half. (Or of course, if you've found a pre-printed chart form you like, use that instead. It may come with an aspect grid, but if not, you'll need to draw a grid yourself.)

Figure 9 on the next page shows an example of an aspect grid form which has not yet been filled in with the symbols for the chart's aspects.

Figure 9

	☉	☽	☿	♀	♂	♃	♄	♅	♆	♇
☉										
☽										
☿										
♀										
♂										
♃										
♄										
♅										
♆										
♇										
Asc										
MC										

So, thinking of this form as a table in a word processing document or a simple spreadsheet, we see that each row is headed with the symbols for each of the planets, and in addition the bottom two rows are headed by the abbreviations for Ascendant and Midheaven respectively.

In each row, we draw in the symbols (glyphs) that represent each aspect made by each planet. The Sun's aspects will occupy the first row across the grid, the next row is for the Moon aspects, the next row is the Mercury aspects, and so on down to the Ascendant and Midheaven at the bottom.

Now looking at it vertically, column by column, we see that each column is also headed with the symbols for each of the planets (but not the ASC and MC this time). Each of these columns gives us a square cell into which to write in the symbols for the aspects that the planets named in the rows make to the planets named in the columns.

To see how it's done, in our example chart we have Sun conjunct Mercury. So, in the top row of the aspect table, draw the glyph for 'conjunction' in the cell where the row that is headed by the symbol for the Sun intersects with the column that is headed by the symbol for Mercury. This now lets us know at a quick glance that the Sun conjuncts Mercury in this chart.

We then follow suit with all of the other planets and their aspects, and end up with a completed grid as per Figure 10:

Figure 10

	⊙	☽	☿	♀	♂	♃	♄	♅	♆	♇
⊙			☌				☍			☍
☽			☍		☌		⚹			
☿							△			
♀						△	□	⚹		
♂			☍				☍	⚹		
♃										
♄										☌
♅										
♆										⚹
♇										
Asc		△		□	△		☍			
MC		△			△	□	⚹			

Now, as a result, you have a nice useful easy-to-refer-to representation of which planet is doing what to which other planet.

And we're done drawing up the example chart! Now read on for further info and how to interpret your newly-drawn chart.

LESS STRAIGHTFORWARD CHARTS

If the birth time is unknown

If the time of birth is completely unknown, you will have to use noon as a hypothetical time of birth and draw up what is called a Solar chart.

In these, the Sun sign is used as the first House and the chart is set up as though 0º of the Sun sign is the Ascendant, and the Houses are not used in the interpretation at all – only the signs and aspects can be used.

Obviously this gives a very limited amount of material from which to interpret, and is why it's so important to have a birth time. When there is no known time of birth, we can not find out the Ascendant, the Midheaven, or the signs of the Houses.

Also, please note that, as you will then have to arbitrarily work with the moon's position at noon, the Moon aspects will probably also not be very accurate. For instance, the Moon's noon position may be many degrees away from where it was at the unknown time of birth.

If the birth time is only approximate

If, for example, the person can only tell you that he/she was born between 4:00am and 5:00am, the best you can do (until you become experienced in doing what is called Rectification, in which you take a brief history of the person's life and use guesswork as to where the most likely planet-House positions would be according to the 'best fit' with the person's past experiences) is to use a halfway time, eg 4:30.

It's necessary to warn the person that the chart may not be totally accurate as far as House position and aspects to the Ascendant and Midheaven go.

Longitudes other than 0

This bit is only for those who are not using Astrolog or other computer software. If you are using Astrolog or similar, skip ahead to 'Part Two: Interpreting The Chart'.

So far we've only dealt with a birth time occurring at GMT in London, at 0º longitude. In other cases, two extra steps need to be taken.

As an example, we'll look at the chart of someone born in New York City, which has a latitude of 40º 43' North and a longitude of 74º 00' West. The birth data are:

- Date of birth: 2 January 1952

- Time of birth: 10:07 p.m. local (New York) time

- Place of birth: New York City

First, the time of birth must be converted to Greenwich Mean Time. As New York's time zone is 5 hours behind GMT, 5 hours are added to the time of birth to obtain the GMT. Therefore, the time of birth in GMT is 3:07 a.m.

Note that in this case we have crossed over past midnight and gone into the following day, so the date of birth will actually now be considered to be 3 January.

The calculations go as follows:

- 12:00 (Noon)

- -3:07 (birth time)

- =8:53 (interval)

Then,

- 18:48.15 (Sidereal time at noon)

- -8:53.00 (interval)

- =9:55.15

And then,

- 9:55.15

- -:01.29 (acceleration on interval)

- =9:53.46 (Sidereal Time at GMT)

Now there's one new calculation to learn: the Longitudinal Equivalent. This is found by multiplying the longitude by 4.

- Multiply 74 (degrees) by 4 = 296.

- Convert this into hours and minutes by dividing by 60:

- 296/60 = 4 hours 56 minutes.

This is then subtracted from Sidereal Time at Greenwich at the time of birth:

- 9:53.46 (Sidereal Time at Greenwich

- -4:56.00 (longitudinal equivalent

- =4:57.46 (local Sidereal Time at time of birth)

It is this local Sidereal Time that we base our chart on. We look up the time of 4:57.46 in a Table of Houses for New York City, and then all procedures are the same as you've already learned.

The longitudinal equivalent also applies to longitudes other than 0° even when there is no 'time zone' difference.

As an example, although Liverpool is in the same time zone as London, it has a longitude of 2° 55'W rather than 0° as London has, and this has to be converted as follows:

- $4 \times 2^{\circ} = 8$

- $4 \times 55' = 220$.

Divide 220 by 60, which gives 3 and a remainder of 40.

Add:

- 8 (minutes)

- 3 (minutes) and 40 (seconds)

- =11 mins. 40 secs.

The result of 11 minutes 40 seconds is then subtracted from Sidereal Time at Greenwich at the time of birth, to give the local Sidereal Time at time of birth.

For longitudes east of 0º, the same procedure is followed as we just followed for Liverpool except the longitudinal equivalent is added instead of subtracted.

Ending up with a sidereal time greater than 24:00

Sometimes at the end of your calculations, you'll find that you've ended up with a local Sidereal Time greater than 24 hours. All you need to do is subtract 24 hours from this result.

For instance, if you arrive at a local Sidereal Time of 27:09.44:

- 27:09.4

- -24:00.0

- =3:09.44

So, 3:09.44 is the time you'll work with.

We've now covered everything needed to draw up a

chart! Now to interpret it.

The next part of this book tells you what each element of a chart means, and sets you on your way to learning how to interpret.

INTERPRETING THE CHART

WHAT EACH CHART ELEMENT MEANS

The Houses

1st House

This describes your basic personality, your appearance, your innermost thoughts. The 'real you'. Any planets found in this House will have an important effect on your personality and often also your appearance.

2nd House

Possessions, money, your ability to earn. Planets in this House indicate (especially by aspect to other planets) whether the acquisition of money and/or possessions is likely to be relatively easy or difficult.

3rd House

Early education, short-distance travel, communication. It also has to do with brothers and sisters, neighbors, and your relationship to your everyday environment.

4th House

The domestic environment and what sort of home conditions are likely to exist. It also signifies the very beginning of our life (our roots, including our parents).

5th House

Creativity of all sorts, whether it be in the sense of creating things (music, a painting, a poem, an acting role, etc.) or in the sense of creating children! This House also has to do with the pleasures of life, such as love affairs, other recreational activities, games and sports.

6th House

Work, the job environment, your workmates, your attitude towards work. It also has to do with health, and any planets found in this House are a possible indication of the subject's state of health and of any specific health problems.

7th House

Marriage and long-term love relationships, plus other types of significant partnerships such as best friend or business partner. The sign on the cusp of this House can often be a representation of the marriage partner; he or she may have the traits associated with that particular sign, or may actually be that Sun sign or have it as their Rising ign.

8th House

Big business, involvement in other people's finances, inheritances, legacies, property, jointly-owned money. It also has to do with sex, the occult, and the after-life.

9th House

Higher education, long-distance travel, foreigners, foreign languages. It also rules serious subjects such as philosophy, law, and religion.

10th House

The profession, your social standing, responsibilities and authority figures. Planets and the sign on the cusp of this House are possible indications of suitable occupations.

11th House

Friendships, acquaintances, social clubs, all group activities. It also covers intellectual pleasures (as opposed to sport and other physical recreations covered by the 5th House).

12th House

The subconscious, dreams, memories, mystical experiences. Solitary pursuits, time spent alone. Challenging aspects to planets in this House may give a tendency towards depression or alcoholism; easy aspects may give psychic or

How To Do Your Own Astrological Chart

spiritual inclinations.

The Planets

The Sun

Your 'Sun Sign'. Your most apparent personality traits and potentials - the basic ones that 'shine' out the most notably and typically.

The Moon

The emotional side of your personality. It reflects the attitudes that were formed in early life by the family and home environment, and determines your instinctive behavior.

Mercury

The intellect, the way you think and communicate. It's also associated with the nervous system and with travel.

Venus

The pleasurable side of life – love, close friendship, social life. It also has to do with the arts, all forms of beauty, and with personal finances.

Mars

Your ambitions, drives, desires. It indicates action, assertiveness and (if it makes challenging aspects) aggression and risk-taking.

Jupiter

Knowledge, higher learning (either via formal education or through life experience), philosophy, religion, foreign travel and languages. Jupiter stands for expansive principles, and can indicate ways in which you can better yourself.

Saturn

'The old taskmaster'. Saturn deals with restrictions and limitations; it shows ways in which you have to learn to accept responsibility and grow in maturity. It represents the lessons you need to learn in life.

Uranus

Originality, individuality, inventiveness, modern-ness. It also signifies sudden occurrences, unexpected events, eccentricity, and rules all things electric.

Neptune

Imagination, sensitivity, spirituality. It is associated with the fine arts, mysticism, and religious inspiration. If it is strong in an individual's chart, it adds a dreamy, mysterious quality, while challenging aspects to it may signify negative escapism.

Pluto

Pluto is associated with change (whether of a voluntary or enforced type), transformation, regeneration. It also represents the fading in and out of conditions.

Ascendant (Rising Sign) and Midheaven

Ascendant (ASC)

A very strong influence, as important as the Sun. It represents your inner self – the way you are when alone. It adds another side to your personality, modifying the traits of the Sun sign.

Midheaven (MC)

Represents the area of the heavens in which the Sun appears at noon. It indicates how others see you, your outward expression, your social standing, your ego. It also has to do with the career.

The Triplicities and Quadruplicities

There are two sets of general characteristics that the signs fall into. These two groups are called **triplicities** and **quadruplicities**.

QUADRUPLICITES

These consist of the four elements Fire, Earth, Air and Water, and the 12 signs are categorized under the four elements as follows:

- **Fire:** Aries, Leo Sagittarius

- **Earth**: Taurus, Virgo, Capricorn

- **Air:** Gemini, Libra, Aquarius

- **Water**: Cancer, Scorpio, Pisces

This is what is meant when someone says 'Taurus is an Earth sign', 'Scorpio is a Water sign', etc.

It's usually found that people born under a particular element will get on well with others of the same element: for instance an Aries will usually get along with a Leo or a Sagittarius.

Each group typifies a certain set of character traits:

Earth: Down-to-earth, practical, self-sufficient, able to take responsibility

Air: Intellectual, may often 'have their head in the clouds', not too emotional

Fire: Self-confident, outgoing, dynamic, fiery, active go-getters

Water: Emotional, sensitive, intuitive, can be dreamy, often creative in some way

The set of traits in question will be more noticeable in a person the more strongly a particular element figures in their chart.

For example, a Gemini with Libra rising and several planets in Air signs will have much more definitely 'Airy' characteristics than a Gemini with Cancer rising and no other planets in Air signs. If our Gemini with Cancer rising had most of his/her planets in Water signs, he/she would actually be more a Water type than an Air type, despite the Air Sun sign.

TRIPLICITIES

- **Cardinal:** Aries, Cancer, Libra, Capricorn

- **Mutable:** Gemini, Virgo, Sagittarius, Pisces

- **Fixed:** Taurus, Leo, Scorpio, Aquarius

Again, these indicate trait tendencies and two people whose signs fall into the same Triplicity will find they usually have traits in common.

Cardinal: Self-motivating, able to take the initiative, action-taking

Mutable: Adaptable, flexible, versatile, changeable

Fixed: Fixed opinions, disliking change, stubborn, persistent

The Aspects

Aspects are angles of varying degrees and fall into two interpretation types: 'good and/or easy' and 'bad and/or challenging'. As you would expect from that description, 'good' aspects create a fortunate influence, while 'bad' ones bring a degree of difficulty in the area concerned.

'Bad' aspects are not always so bad, nor 'good' ones so good, as they may at first appear. Loads of trines and sextiles in someone's chart may actually be not such a good thing for them, as this may result in someone who gets a bit spoiled by frequent good luck and doesn't build the amount of character and resourcefulness necessary to guide them through hard times if and when they occur.

Conversely, many squares and oppositions in a chart can indicate the presence of a lot of bad luck throughout life, but this also can strengthen character and determination, and provide the extra challenge to spur that person on to achieve greatness. So do take the person's whole character and attitude into account when deciding how to interpret the aspects.

NOTE: For the sake of simplicity in this beginner's book, we will only cover the most major aspects, which exert the strongest influence. There are other less significant aspects that you can learn about later (such as the semi-square, semi-sextile and so on), but as those exert a very minimal effect, we will stick to only the most noticeable and clear-cut ones for this book.

Conjunction

0º apart, 8º orb: Usually a 'good' aspect, but conjunctions can be either good or challenging depending on the two planets involved

and where they are in the chart, and whether other planets make aspects to the conjunction. In any case, a conjunction is always a strong focal point.

Sextile

60º apart, 5º orb: 'Good' aspect. Moderately helpful, representing a pleasant flow between the two planets.

Square

90º apart, 8º orb: 'Bad' aspect. A very challenging aspect, this indicates tension or difficulty between the two areas that are represented by the planets, signs and Houses involved.

Trine

120º apart, 8º orb: 'Good' aspect. This is the most helpful aspect to have, indicating a very smooth flow between the signs, Houses and planets involved.

Quincunx

150º apart, 2º orb: 'Bad' aspect. A mildly challenging aspect, indicating an area of some strain or difficulty.

Opposition

180º apart, 8º orb: 'Bad' aspect. As its name suggests, it signifies opposing forces in the chart. Can indicate a polarity of some sort, a feeling of being pulled in two different directions according to the signs, planets and Houses involved.

A SAMPLE INTERPRETATION

Now we'll look at a small extract from a real chart interpretation, to see how what we've learned fits together. This is based on our example chart for 7th April 1982 that we've been working on.

My own style of writing up my chart interpretations is to do it in three parts: the first on 'Personality', the second on 'Work and Finances', and the third on 'Relationships'. You can follow suit, or else just go with whatever way of organizing your interpretation seems right for you.

The example extract given below is from the 'Personality' section that I would write for my own chart interpretations.

To find out about 'Relationships', you look at Venus, its aspects, the sign it's in, and the House it's in. Then the Seventh House, the sign on the Seventh House cusp, planets in the Seventh House and any aspects they may make, which all give suggestions about a type of partner. The Fifth House can give indications to do with love affairs and children. For friendships, look at the Eleventh House, Venus, and Jupiter.

For 'Work and Finances', look to the Tenth House: look at the sign on this House, the planets in it, and the aspects to planets in it, for the possible profession. Look in the Sixth House for work conditions, the Second for finances, the Eighth for matters to do with inheritances, legal and/or big business issues, and sometimes the Midheaven can give a suggestion of a suitable type of career.

Additionally, travel comes under the Third House (short journeys), the Ninth House (long journeys), and Mercury.

AN EXAMPLE EXTRACT

Looking again at our example birth chart, we see that the Sun is in Aries in the 11th House. So, a write-up for the 'Personality' section of the interpretation can start something like this simple example, which blends the qualities of Sun in Aries and Sun in 11th House:

SUN IN ARIES IN 11th HOUSE gives you energy and enthusiasm. Arians like to be first and best in everything they do, and they can have leadership potential, enjoying the recognition it can bring. You're likely to be adventurous, with plenty of courage. Impatience can be a problem for you; you may need to think things out more before doing them (Arians tend to do things on impulse!).

Your main possible negative trait is that of always putting yourself first – if that's the case, you need to think in terms of considering others more and remembering that they may have something valuable to input too.

It's likely you have many friends and enjoy social activities and being part of a group. Your friendships are of a particularly rewarding type, and other people feel that your presence adds fun and happiness to the occasion.

We also find that in this chart, the Sun makes three aspects: conjunction with Mercury, opposition with Saturn, and opposition with Pluto. So, the interpretation will continue as follows:

SUN CONJUNCT MERCURY emphasizes creative potential. You have a great deal of mental energy, but need to be careful that this combination doesn't drive you to become 'burnt out' through overwork.

SUN OPPOSE SATURN may indicate a need to take on some heavy responsibilities at some point in life. You can find that you seem to need to work harder than others to achieve your ambitions. But if you do achieve them, they will be particularly worthwhile.

SUN OPPOSE PLUTO shows a very forceful manner; you may try too hard to make others see your point of view and to share your opinions, and this may be off-putting for some, so try to tone it down a bit if you see that this is happening. A need to find a good positive way to 'let off steam' is likely!

Next, we move along to interpret the Rising Sign and the Moon:

GEMINI RISING shows that you enjoy reading, travel and communication. You're talkative, an energetic and entertaining speaker, and may have considerable writing talent as well. You like to know at least a little about virtually every subject (others may think of you as a goldmine of information), and you enjoy sharing your knowledge with others.

MOON IN LIBRA IN 4th HOUSE shows a tactful manner, which helps balance out the Arian's natural tendency towards self-centeredness! This position of the Moon helps make you easy-going and friendly, making for popularity with others. You have an emotional need for approval from other people. You're sociable and your home may be a popular base for social events.

See how it works? And so on, down to Pluto in its sign and House, and its various aspects. You just assemble together the meanings of each planet, sign, House and aspect, in order to create a cohesive interpretation.

PART TWO: INTERPRETATION

This is where the instructional part of the book ends and the database begins. From here on, the remainder of this book consists solely of a big reference database of the meanings of the signs, planets, Houses and aspects. Come here for all of the individual interpretations for every component found in a chart.

As you become more experienced at doing charts and get more conversant with each of these components, you'll get better at blending them with the other elements of the chart rather than seeing each as a separate entity, so that it will all start to flow together nicely.

PLANETS IN THE SIGNS
SUN SIGNS

SUN IN ARIES (21/22 March to 19/20 April, ruling planet Mars)

Aries is the first sign of the zodiac, and that is the key to the character of Aries. His/her philosophy of life can be summed up in the key phrase 'Me first!' Arians want to be the first and best in everything. They can be incredibly energetic and enthusiastic, sometimes to the point of driving others up the wall! They're courageous and adventurous. The quickness of the Aries mind is rarely at a loss for words, particularly those of a sharp, witty variety.

They hate rigid routine, becoming restless and bored easily. They can be forever starting new projects that they soon get fed up with, abandon everything, and start on something else.

Novelty wears off very quickly for them.

Arians tend to be hasty, jumping to conclusions and acting without thinking – as a result, they always seem to be getting in trouble of one sort or another. Risk-taking and restlessness are Aries foibles, and they're forever acquiring cuts, burns and head injuries. They suffer headaches and sinus problems more than most, and can be basically quite accident-prone.

They are outspoken, direct and blunt in speech, and tactlessness can sometimes be a 'feature' with them. They may also make hasty claims based on their own opinions without having facts to back them up. But they are not blind to the truth, and if their errors are pointed out to them, these Rams usually acknowledge their mistakes with a sheepish grin, and quickly change the subject!

SUN IN TAURUS (20/21 April to 20/21 May, ruling planet Venus)

Taurus is the most practical, down-to-earth sign. Fond of luxury and good living, Taureans like money and possessions, and lots of them. Not just for the sake of having them (as can be the case with some Cancers and Capricorns) but for the sheer pleasure it brings to use and enjoy them. Taureans also have a great love of good food and some can be prone to having a spot of bother with their weight as a result.

They are warm-hearted, affectionate, often endearing, and tend to be reliable, so can be very good friends to have. But be careful not to cross them, as they usually possess rather a ferocious temper. Their temper is slow to be aroused, but when it is, it's as if all hell has broken loose and the phrase 'bull in a china shop' distinctly comes to mind.

Taureans, being ruled by Venus, can be artistically inclined. This is especially true of music, and many a Taurus can be a fine singer. Sculpture may also appeal to them, giving the Earth sign Taurus an opportunity to work with clay – a substance, after all, from the earth. (Tauruses are probably the ones most likely to have enjoyed making mud pies as children.)

There is a strong need to feel safe and secure. They are usually able to fulfill this need, as they normally have a good head for business and financial matters. Their main potentially difficult point is stubbornness: once a Bull makes up his/her mind, you'll have a hard time changing it.

They are very good at planning, sometimes plodding on for years in an unsatisfactory situation in order to attain some goal – and they are often successful in reaching it. Patience and willpower are very much Taurean values.

SUN IN GEMINI (21/22 May to 21/22 June, ruling planet Mercury)

Gemini has more to do with the intellect, the mental processes, than any other sign. They enjoy reading, writing, radio, TV, any form of communication. They also love to talk, and are usually lively, witty speakers.

They're capable of, and enjoy, doing several things at a time. A Gemini can be quite happy eating, reading, watching TV and surfing the Net all while keeping up a conversation with one or more people. This also results in the common Gemini tendency to keep starting new projects (often more than one at a time), abandoning them, and starting several other things (also, as you've seen, often a problem for Arians). They can be going in all different directions at once, unable to make up their minds quite what to do with themselves.

They often go through several different careers before settling down to one they feel they can live with. And even then, they can get fed up with that one pretty quickly.

They have an insatiable appetite for knowledge, and usually learn speedily and easily. Geminis particularly like to learn at least a little about every conceivable subject (and some pretty inconceivable ones) and enjoy showing off their learnedness.

Geminis have a need for continual change and have a strong general restlessness, both of which make them specially fond of travel. They like to be on the go.

Their main negative features can be those of shallowness and fickleness; some may need to stop and think how the other person is feeling.

One great feature is that Geminis tend to stay looking young and thinking young all their lives, an asset many will envy!

SUN IN CANCER (22/23 June to 22/23 July, ruling planet the Moon)

Cancer is the most 'domesticated' sign. Those born under it tend to be the most home-loving and family-orientated of the signs. Cancerians are very protective towards family and loved ones, having a strong maternal or paternal instinct. A real home is very important for them - they are often the ones who are the first among your friends to buy their own homes and furnish them lovingly.

Sensitive and easily hurt, they withdraw into their shells at the smallest slight. They present a hard exterior, like the crab shell, but, also like the crab, are really soft inside. They can be hard to fathom at times, prone to mood swings.

Cancerians have great imaginations, and are also great worriers – and it can be the great imagination that contributes to the great worrying! They're prone to digestive upsets as a result of worry.

They usually have excellent memories, able to surprise others with their ability to recall events from their early childhood, and are good at remembering historical dates (history is often one of their favorite subjects). Cancers are patriotic creatures, feeling pride in their country and in their own roots.

A talent for cooking is a likely Cancer trait, and many can go on to become accomplished chefs. A favorite hobby is collecting things, which could manifest itself in a beautiful collection of art objects, or, on the other hand, a house or flat jammed with paper bags, string, etc.

SUN IN LEO (23/24 July to 22/23 August, ruling planet the Sun)

Here we have the 'King' of the zodiac. Leos like to be the boss, and are happiest when they have their own kingdom to rule - whether this be a country, or a circle of friends or workmates. They love drama, and take great glee in playing the part of a member of the nobility.

Leos are born actors, loving to show off. They crave adulation, and any career that puts them on display for all to admire, suits them to a T. You will find many Leos in show business, sports, and any other profession that puts them in the public eye.

They are kind and generous people, provided that you stay in your place and not try to usurp the kingly throne. Leos are sensitive and are easily hurt when their regal dignity is affronted. If you stay on the correct side and give them a good ego-stroking, however, they make enormously loyal friends.

Leonians have much creative potential, and if they choose to follow a creative career or hobby they usually find that they have no lack of inspirational new ideas. Their thought processes are not necessarily quick, but they are steady.

Leo's main faults can be those of pomposity and of being too fixed in their ideas and opinions. They need to try to see things from others' point of view. At their worst, they can be conceited, power-mad bullies - but when they're GOOD, they can truly bring a 'ray of sunshine' into others' lives.

SUN IN VIRGO (23/24 August to 22/23 September, ruling planet Mercury)

There's only one sign that is more of a worry-wart than Cancer, and that is Virgo. Virgos are logic orientated and perfectionist, and some can be obsessive. If their lives don't fall into a secure, predictable pattern, they can get very worried indeed. They can be highly-strung, their health suffering if they don't achieve positive release of their nervous tension.

Virgos have great analytical sense and a keen eye for

69

detail, suiting them for specially intricate, complicated types of work that less focused people shy away from. They can be hard workers, and their desire to be of service to others can make them good doctors, nurses, social workers, teachers; any profession dedicated to helping others.

They're usually interested in health matters, especially diet. They often follow healthy, wholefood diets, having a dislike of junk food.

Virgoans are sometimes thought of as prudish in emotional relationships, but in fact they are capable of very deep feeling, just needing someone to help bring them out, as they tend to be shy about showing their feelings (especially the more Virgo someone has in his/her chart). The main problem is their perfectionism – it's hard to find someone to measure up to their pernickety standards! Learning that we all (even Virgos themselves) have out faults, can help them to overcome this stumbling-block.

SUN IN LIBRA (23/24 September to 22/23 October, ruling planet Venus)

Libras are the charmers of the zodiac. Tactful, considerate, easy-going, they tend to be well-liked and popular. Needing to find beauty, harmony and balance in all things, they hate unpleasantness and quarrels and will often go out of their way to avoid them.

As they are ruled by Venus, they also, like their fellow Venus-ruled Taurus, are fond of the arts, especially music, and are often talented in them. As Libra is an Air sign while Taurus is an Earth sign, Libran art or music is likely to be more intellectual or cerebral, while Taurean art/music will be more of an earthy, gritty type.

They need pleasant living conditions, and will strive to make their homes as comfortable and pleasing to the eye as possible. They like to entertain at home and are good at making guests feel relaxed and at keeping them entertained. Librans have a powerful natural instinct for partnership; they need a marriage or good friendship of an especially close type, a soul mate to share their lives with, in order to feel fulfilled and happy.

Libra's main problems are indecisiveness and a lethargic streak. They can see all sides of a problem too well, resulting in inability to make up their minds as to which is the right one. They have a strong sense of justice and don't want to run the risk of seeing anyone treated unfairly.

SUN IN SCORPIO (23/24 October to 21/22 November, ruling planet Pluto)

Scorpio is the most intense, passionate sign, not just in romance or sex matters (the subjects most popularly associated with the sign) but in everything they do: work, play, hobbies, anything that interests them. They throw themselves into things with an all-consuming fervor, needing to live life to the fullest.

These are the people who possess those 'piercing' eyes, often either clear icy blue or dark brown-black. Scorpios have a mysterious intensity, a strong personal magnetism that can be irresistibly attractive.

Scorpions can follow either of two paths: they have been described as capable of either soaring to the heights of spirituality (sometimes represented by the eagle rather than the scorpion) or sinking to the depths of depravity. And they can be perfectly capable of following either course to the fullest extent!

Their main fault is that of jealousy, and they are also inclined to holding grudges. When angry with you, they will go back over years and years of the deep dark past to bring up every little slight, real or imagined, you've ever perpetrated upon them: 'Oh, yeah? Remember twenty years ago when you said...' (some innocent statement, possibly about the weather, that you had completely forgotten and never meant in the way they took it anyway).

They have a love of the mysterious, of delving into hidden depths. Scorpios are exceedingly imaginative and intuitive, and are good at anticipating the thoughts of others.

SUN IN SAGITTARIUS (22/23 November - 21/22 December, ruling planet Jupiter)

Sagittarians are freedom-loving and adventurous. They love to travel, especially abroad, and are the sign most likely to take up residence far from their place of birth. They are fascinated by foreign language and culture, and by foreigners themselves.

They may enjoy indulging in deep and intensive study just for the sake of it, especially of philosophy and other serious subjects. Their intellectual capacity can be considerable. They get bored easily and, like their opposite sign Gemini, are happiest when they can chop and change, either working on several different projects at the same time or changing rapidly from one project to another.

Sagittarians hate even the slightest whiff of restriction or repression, and will fight against these with determination. They need to feel that they retain a certain amount of freedom within their relationships and their domestic environments; they can find ordinary family-orientated home life too mundane.

Fondness for outdoor activities and for sport are typical traits. Horseback riding often appeals to these Centaurs – if not, there is at least a love of animals in general and possibly horses in particular.

They are not big on worrying, but can tend toward blind recklessness and may exaggerate things. Restlessness is also likely to be a trying trait for them. But, if the Sagittarian can channel all this excess energy into a positive outlet, he/she can accomplish much.

SUN IN CAPRICORN (22/23 December to 19 January, ruling planet Saturn)

These are the ambitious ones: always wanting to get things accomplished, always trying to better themselves materially, mentally, spiritually, or all three. They desire to reach the top in their chosen field, and to be admired for it, and they will work long and hard to attain that goal. Driven by the need for recognition, they are capable of throwing their entire personalities into their careers.

Capricorns often have musical ability (especially if Taurus, Libra or Venus are strong in the chart) and are keen readers. They usually have a good sense of humor, most notably of a dry, ironic type.

They can be pessimistic and cynical, tending to look on the dark side of things. Indeed, the poor old Goats are the most prone to depression of all the signs. They tend to feel alone a lot of the time.

There is a distinct characteristic they have of being 'old when young and young when old' – they have a seriousness and maturity in childhood that makes them seem like old people in children's bodies, yet as they get older they seem to become more youthful (and less gloomy) in outlook. Often, they can be sickly in youth but gain better health in adulthood, generally living to a ripe old age.

They like learning things through practical experience rather than through dry study, although they are well capable of both. And whatever they learn is digested thoroughly and never forgotten, in the hope that it can be utilized at some point in accomplishing something worthwhile.

SUN IN AQUARIUS (20 January to 18/19 February, ruling planet Uranus)

Independent, original, and often somewhat eccentric - these are the most notable traits associated will the sign Aquarius. People often don't know just what to make of an Aquarian; he/she can seem unpredictable and full of surprises.

They are usually humanitarian in nature, sometimes devoting themselves to helpful causes, and are very friendly – but both the humanitarianism and the friendliness are carried out in a detached sort of way. That is, they like to be amiable, approachable and helpful, but don't like to get too emotionally involved.

Aquarians are sociable, wanting to surround themselves with other people, disliking being alone. Social events are very important to them; they want to be part of a group.

The Aquarian has an original, inventive mind. They tend to be broad-minded and will try new and different things. They're usually intelligent and intellectually inclined, and are quick to learn though their rate of learning can be erratic. Their interests are invariably unusual ones, often to do with science in one form or another.

Even the more conventional interests will be unconventional in the hands of an Aquarian: if they like art, it will be avant-garde art; if music, it will be ultra-modern and maybe electronic, not too much of the violins and French horns.

SUN IN PISCES (19/20 February - 20/21 March, ruling planet Neptune)

The most sensitive and emotional of the signs, Pisceans are truly compassionate and sympathetic souls. They have a sincere desire to help others, to relieve suffering, even if it requires some measure of inconvenience to themselves.

They can not handle too much unpleasant reality, however. If things get too much for them they run off and escape, sometimes by way of alcohol, drugs or both – Pisces has a stronger tendency than other signs to escape in this less than ideal way and they can do themselves a big favor by finding a positive outlet of escape instead – the arts, particularly dancing and imaginative writing, are good examples.

Pisces is symbolized by two fishes swimming in opposite directions, and the Piscean often personifies this image. They can seem chaotic – their thought processes work in a way that can leave non-Pisceans confused. They're intuitive, have brilliant imaginations and can do great creative work if they can just sit themselves down and get organized.

Pisceans are very likeable. They usually have a wacky sense of humor, winning others over with quirky off-the-wall ways of looking at things and with whimsically silly remarks

(Pisces is a good sign for professional comedians). In emotional relationships, they are romantic and sentimental.

Some may feel attracted towards the psychic sciences, with mediumship and spiritual healing being of particular interest, but in any case, they can show a seemingly telepathic sense of empathy with others, sometimes 'just knowing' what someone is going to say next, or finishing someone's sentence for them.

MOON SIGNS

MOON IN ARIES

The 'Me first!' philosophy takes on a highly emotional aspect when the Moon is in this sign. The person with Moon in Aries tends to dominate others emotionally (though often in a charming way). They are willful types, not heeding the advice of others and insisting on doing things their own way, even if notably wrong! There is a good deal of enthusiasm and impulsiveness.

Sudden attacks of temper can also be a feature of these individuals, especially if there are challenging aspects to the Moon.

MOON IN TAURUS

This is considered the best sign for the Moon to be in; the stability of Taurus helps to steady the changeability associated with the Moon.

The Moon here is often good for financial matters, material comfort and security. There's love of, and maybe talent in, the arts. This Moon helps add ability to see projects through to the end, which is a good influence for those with Sun or Ascendant in a restless sign like Gemini or Aries.

MOON IN GEMINI

People with the Moon here may be changeable and restless in mood; their emotional nature can be inconsistent and give mixed signals to others. They're often restless physically as well, taking many trips and maybe changing residence more frequently than most.

They can be highly strung and may talk a lot through nervousness. Quick-witted and versatile, they enjoy reading and like being knowledgeable about a lot of different subjects.

MOON IN CANCER

Strong family instinct appears in those with the Moon in this sign, a need to cherish, nourish, and protect. Emotional level is high, and imagination strong. They usually make excellent homemakers and parents (though with challenging aspects to the Moon, they may possibly be a little too emotional or overprotective).

There's sensitivity to others' moods and feelings, and empathy. These people can be very caring and nurturing, but need to be careful not to be too clinging.

MOON IN LEO

They love the spotlight, having an emotional need to be admired and appreciated by all. They're consumed with needing to love and be loved; they are warm-hearted, romantic souls. Their dispositions are usually sunny and they are self-confident and affectionate.

Fondness for luxury and sophisticated entertainment is present, such as for theatre, concerts, fancy meals out. But watch out, if there are challenging aspects to the Moon, they can be bossy, self-indulgent prima donnas! They're fond of children, and are very loyal.

MOON IN VIRGO

There's a tendency to worry quite a lot, especially about the emotional side of life. Often those with the Moon here are a bit on the shy and retiring side, maybe a little nervous, but much like the Moon-Cancerians they possess great capacity for being of service to their loved ones and to nurture them.

Health and good diet are often of interest and importance to them, and they may be vegetarians and/or attracted to alternative forms of medicine.

MOON IN LIBRA

The Moon here gives charm and grace. Friendly and sociable, these people are well-liked – which is just as well, as Moon-Librans feel that their emotional well-being depends on the approval of others! There's distaste for disharmony, coarseness and vulgarity, any sort of unpleasantness.

Entertaining in the home is of great enjoyment and benefit, and they desire to be surrounded by good friends as much of the time as possible rather than being on their own. But they need to not be too emotionally dependent on others.

MOON IN SCORPIO

There is a serious attitude towards the emotional side of things. Their emotions run high, although these are usually kept fairly well controlled. If they can find positive things to channel their considerable emotional energies into, they can accomplish much of real value.

When a Moon-Scorpion feels they have been insulted or betrayed, jealousy and resentment can quickly seethe and erupt. Even a small slight (real or imagined) can bring forth an unexpected eruption of sharp-tongued nastiness. Like the Sun-Scorpio, they can hold grudges for a very long time.

MOON IN SAGITTARIUS

With the Moon here, there's the need for some degree of freedom and independence within all types of relationships. They're not good at settling down to follow an everyday domestic routine. Restlessness and recklessness are likely, and a good outlet for the Moon-Sagittarian abundance of emotional energy is through sport and/or exercise.

People with this Moon position tend to be fluent of speech and quick of movement, and some like changing residence frequently. Foreign travel usually appeals on an emotional level, and quite a few of those with this Moon sign will emigrate and set up home abroad.

MOON IN CAPRICORN

Emotionally reserved and cautious are the keywords for those with the Moon here. They may appear aloof – they (and friends and loved ones) need to work on breaking down this wall of reserve to bring out the real human being behind it. Some may let the financial/material side of life take precedence over the emotional.

They're enduringly loyal to their family and their true friends, will help them out financially if and when they can, and usually have good common sense.

MOON IN AQUARIUS

They like to be unconventional in their emotional relationships; they're likely to have friends who are unusual in some way or who are even considered pretty odd! There are likely to be masses of acquaintances, most of whom the Moon-Aquarian doesn't feel really close to, but just likes to have a lot of people around. He or she may have only one or two important friends, and if there are challenging aspects to the Moon they may be a little afraid of emotional involvement.

In any case, however, they're always friendly and willing to help. This can often manifest in very constructive ways, such as working for humanitarian causes.

MOON IN PISCES

People with the Moon here are very receptive and sensitive emotionally. They're kind and gentle, often a little shy, and can be very vulnerable. As with Moon in Scorpio, their emotional level is high; they sometimes get quite carried away. Imagination is usually strong and often there's talent for art, music or poetic writing.

Compassion and sympathy are strong traits with them, and they are generally very romantic, maybe a little dreamy. They're easily hurt, often through blindness to others' bad traits – they can tend to see others as nicer or better than they really are. If other factors in the chart support it, there may be psychic ability.

MERCURY SIGNS

MERCURY IN ARIES

These people are quick-thinking, witty, and outspoken (maybe even too outspoken at times!). They're impatient and sometimes will make rash decisions just to 'get on with it', which sometimes lands them in trouble.

Love of argument and debate is usually evident. There is abundance of mental energy and the mind is imaginative and inventive.

MERCURY IN TAURUS

Here we find a practical and steady mentality, with common sense and business sense. They're able to plod along at routine tasks that others find hellishly boring, in order to attain a well-thought-out and much cherished goal.

There's love of the arts and music, and often ability in them as well. Singing and/or songwriting could be a notable talent, especially if the Sun is in Taurus as well.

MERCURY IN GEMINI

This is usually the mark of the chatterbox – someone who enjoys chatting at length, in great detail, and very rapidly, about everything under the sun. The mind is ingenious and versatile, with a need to learn as much as possible.

They can be very interesting to talk to, being a storehouse of all sorts of information. Although, on the other side of the coin, sometimes they may be the sort of people who waffle on and on without ever actually saying anything! The excess mental energy bestowed upon those with Mercury here can sometimes cause nervous tension; they need to learn to relax.

MERCURY IN CANCER

There is usually an excellent memory and imagination, and probably a tendency to worry. The thinking of Mercury-Cancerians is affected by that of their friends and family, and it can often be easy to sway them by appealing to their emotions. Sensitive and sympathetic, they often can be found feeling sorry both for others and themselves.

They may live much in the past, though this can manifest in a positive way, as a flair for knowledge about history. Much thought is given to the home and family and other domestic stuff.

MERCURY IN LEO

Here we have a strong-minded individual capable of power and purpose. They can be good at organizing and at carrying responsibility, and like to be seen as figures of authority (though those with challenging Mercury aspects may be somewhat autocratic!).

There can be ability for the performing arts, especially acting of a dramatic or melodramatic sort. They're self-confident and good at tackling problems. Having a love of children, they can possess a gift for teaching them and bring out the best in them.

MERCURY IN VIRGO

This combination gives an analytical, critical mind, sometimes maybe a little too critical, in the sense of going around finding fault with everything and everyone. If applied positively, however, these qualities can be put to worthwhile use in precision work, detailed scientific or mathematical work, or research.

Medical matters often interest Mercury-Virgoans, and they can also make good computer programmers or technicians. They usually learn quickly and easily.

MERCURY IN LIBRA

In Libra we find a striving for harmony in everything. Desiring always to be just and fair, they can see all sides of a problem, and they always try to construct a solution that will produce the most harmonious outcome for everyone.

Those with Mercury here work best in partnership, the other person often acting as the stimulus to nudge them from inertia and indecision into definite action. Effort must be applied toward an irresistible tendency to always put things off until the last minute.

MERCURY IN SCORPIO

This gives a shrewd and intuitive mind. They are outspoken and direct and believe in saying exactly what they mean – even if it's to the consternation of others! Sarcasm can be a notable trait for them, especially if Mercury has some challenging aspects.

They are willful and determined to rise above the highest obstacle or to delve into the murkiest depths to achieve their goals. They're fascinated with mysterious things, liking a good mystery and doing a bit of sleuthing.

MERCURY IN SAGITTARIUS

Mercury here gives the 'eternal student', someone always in need of intellectual stimulation and new learning. They're able to learn quickly, but can experience mental restlessness so they need to discipline themselves to focus their attention.

There's often a whimsical quality to the way they express themselves – they can be very funny in a zany sort of way. As with Mercury in Scorpio, they're honest and straightforward in speech, and can speak impulsively without considering the consequences. Enjoyment of long-distance travel is likely.

MERCURY IN CAPRICORN

A cool, logical and rational mind is the usual result of Mercury here. Their thinking is practical and realistic, down-to-earth and aware. Methodical and calculating, scientific and mathematical – Star Trek's Mr. Spock comes to mind! They can be good at science-related and/or technical work.

Some may seem a bit stuffy and wet-blankety, but they often possess a great dry sense of humor with an ironic and satirical edge.

MERCURY IN AQUARIUS

Original, forward-looking – 'ahead of their time' is a phrase that can be used to describe many with Mercury here. There's usually eager interest in ultra-modern, high-tech stuff, and the downright weird. Modern science, computers, outer space and astrology are likely to interest Mercury-Aquarians.

Their minds are open and willing to assimilate new and unusual experiences. Many like to work as part of a group, inspiring others with their vision and receiving inspiration back in return.

MERCURY IN PISCES

Mercury here gives an imaginative, impressionable mind plus a high intuitive level. There's usually a good sense of humor, a sense of the absurd, and there can be talent for entertaining others. They can be absent-minded, and their thinking processes may sometimes seem howlingly illogical to those with a more concrete way of thinking.

The fine arts and/or dancing may appeal, and these people may have ability in these subjects. Photography is often a talent when Mercury or the Moon are in this sign.

VENUS SIGNS

VENUS IN ARIES

Although the 'me first!' principle of Aries operates here, when Venus-Arians are truly in love there is still the ability to give as well as take. They enjoy displaying affection to their loved one, having difficulty restraining themselves, along with a very sweet inclination to give unexpected little gifts.

They fall in love quickly in head-over-heels fashion, sparing no effort in their relentless pursuit. They're swashbuckling types and they put lots of vigor and energy into their love life!

VENUS IN TAURUS

The affections are steady and lasting. They have all-consuming need for security and stability in their love lives and are very possessive towards their partners ('You're mine - all MINE!' is a true Venus in Taurus phrase). Jealousy of the enraged-bull type usually follows if they feel the relationship is threatened.

They are very sensual, enjoying lots of physical contact

with their partners, and they give and receive affection happily. There is love of comfort and luxury, of personal beauty and beautiful clothes. Love of the arts, especially music, is likely, and some can have talent in those directions.

VENUS IN GEMINI

Venus is at its most flighty and flirtatious here, with a liking for variety. This is where we find a lot of the Casanovas of the zodiac. Their curiosity about people makes it hard for them to form a permanent relationship with just one, at least not until later in life when they've got much of this curiosity out of their system.

When a Venus-Gemini does get romantically involved, though, they need someone who is intellectual, interesting, intriguing and 'not just a pretty face' – someone that can keep them guessing.

VENUS IN CANCER

A Venus-Cancerian cherishes their partner, giving sincere affection and caring. They cling to their loved ones and try to make the best possible home for them. Often, they like to entertain their partner at home with a lovingly-prepared meal rather than go out on the town – they are likely to be excellent cooks and to have made their home a place of comfort and refuge.

This sign combination is usually indicative of a very domesticated person. They can be moody, but having a secure and stable home helps to keep them balanced.

VENUS IN LEO

These are those dramatic lovers who want to put the object of their affection on a pedestal – that is, provided said object can measure up to their demanding standards! Venus-Leos like a glamorous partner who can be shown off to, and admired by, all (well, the King has to have a Queen, and vice-versa.)

They're romantic, warm-hearted, affectionate, and capable of being very loyal. They expect (demand) the same in return, having a strong psychological need to be appreciated and admired, and to be given utmost loyalty. They are very generous towards their partner, sometimes to the point of giving themselves financial problems!

VENUS IN VIRGO

Venus here may be difficult if the critical/analytical traits of Virgo are applied toward the loved one: the partner's minor faults can be seen as major shortcomings, creating stress within the relationship. They need to be aware of this tendency and realize their lovers are only human and that we all have our faults!

Once this has been sorted out, Venus-Virgoans can give true devotion, being sympathetic, helpful and nurturing towards their partner: they are the ones to tuck up a sick partner in bed and bring them hot soup and make sure the pillows are fluffed up enough.

VENUS IN LIBRA

A happy love relationship is of prime importance to those with Venus here; their need for a partner in order to feel complete is stronger than it is for other Venus positions. Harmony in relationships is essential. They can't stand arguments or other unpleasantness.

They're romantic and affectionate with a desire to please, and seek a partner with whom a specially close bond is possible. As with Venus in Taurus, these individuals will often have an aptitude for music.

VENUS IN SCORPIO

Venus here makes romantic emotions run high! Love is taken very seriously, with a real 'all or nothing' attitude. They won't settle for making do with a partner who isn't 100% right for them (they can feel this in their bones) and will climb the highest mountain or ascend the murkiest depths to find Mr/Ms Right.

It has to be earthshaking, not a light-hearted relationship as with Venus in Gemini or Aquarius, nor the 'comfy' sort enjoyed by Taurus or Cancer Venusians. There must be a real BOIIINNGG effect or it's just not worth it! Once in love, they're loyal and devoted. That is, so long as they're not scorned – if they are, you'd better run. Fast.

VENUS IN SAGITTARIUS

They often don't settle down until later in life, mainly to do with need for freedom combined with high idealism about prospective partners. They're jokey and light-hearted in relationships (maybe not so much if Scorpio is the Sun sign) and like 'horsing around' with their loved one.

They're honest about their feelings. They may be attracted to educated and/or philosophical types or to foreigners, or a combination of all three.

VENUS IN CAPRICORN

They are cautious in their relationships. Some may seem a little aloof and reserved, but very often under the surface is a warm and cuddly human after all. They just don't like to display their feelings publicly, finding it all rather undignified.

It's often the case that, when they marry young, they seek an older, more mature and stable sort of person, and when they marry at a more advanced age, they may do so with someone considerably younger upon whom they can bestow stability and security.

VENUS IN AQUARIUS

Venus here may indicate someone fairly unemotional (maybe less so with Sun in Pisces). Their relationships can be unconventional and involve maintaining a degree of freedom. As with other Air signs, they like a partner who's mentally stimulating, maybe nonconformist. There's dislike of jealousy or possessiveness, and excessive emotionalism really embarrasses them.

As Aquarius is a fixed sign, they are loyal when they make a true love match. It's just a matter of finding someone dynamic enough to keep them intrigued while still giving them freedom to come and go.

VENUS IN PISCES

Venus is considered to be in its best position here: pure, unrelenting love is possible. They're sensitive, very romantic, sentimental, and can be easily moved to tears. Like Venus-Scorpions, they sacrifice all for their loved ones. And, they need to be loved in return, feeling lonely and despondent if this is not forthcoming.

They can be deceived by those who try to take advantage (they often see others as nicer than they really are), so they need to learn to ensure that they go into relationships with eyes open.

MARS SIGNS

MARS IN ARIES

There is urge to take action, to take the initiative, when Mars is in this sign. Energy's abundant and these people can be irrepressible. Those with Mars here want to get out and do things, get stuff accomplished. Often there's leadership ability and they can spark enthusiasm in others.

They're willful and forthright, with dislike of interference by others. They may be accident-prone, especially for Mars-ruled injuries (cuts, burns, head injuries). There's often fondness for fast cars, and sex drive is likely to be strong

MARS IN TAURUS

Stubbornness is the strong trait here. Of course, on the other side of that coin is great perseverance and staying power. They may be slow to react to things, but once they do, they stick to their chosen course with determination.

A tendency towards a formidable temper sometimes appears in those with Mars here: slow to be aroused, but when it goes, get yourself somewhere else immediately! In calmer times, they are affectionate and sensuous while tending to be possessive. Sore throats may be a problem.

MARS IN GEMINI

This placing gives mental energy, sometimes maybe even a little too much: mental restlessness and scattering of intellectual energies can be problematic. They're mentally aggressive, good at debate, and talkative. They enjoy all forms of communication and some may have writing talent.

There's usually lack of patience, with a tendency to keep starting new projects which then get abandoned halfway through. Frequent changes of job are likely; and some may hold down more than one job at the same time.

MARS IN CANCER

Those with Mars here have intense emotions and can be moody. Intuitive ability may be strong. They have a forceful and energetic attitude towards their homes, liking to engage in DIY activities to improve the domestic ambience. People with Mars here can be energetic and enthusiastic parents, trying to spur their kids on to be achievers.

Ambition, action-taking and tenacity are generally evident. Challenging aspects to Mars in such an emotional sign may make some of these people a bit quarrelsome, and may give an inclination towards stomach upsets.

MARS IN LEO

This is a good position for those who would like to be performing artists, as Mars here gives ability to throw energy and enthusiasm into creative and dramatic expression. High-spirited pride and self-confidence are usually found, but care needs to be taken (especially if there are challenging aspects to Mars) not to get too carried away with self-admiration!

There's usually strong attraction both to and from opposite sex, and Mars-Leonians can be persistent pursuers of the object of their affections.

MARS IN VIRGO

Here we often find a wonderfully focused type of person: this sign combination often produces highly-skilled, precise craftspeople who take true pride in their work. They're perfectionist and critical, though they can be a little too fussy about tiny details, sometimes losing sight of the overall picture. They're cautious and systematic in their methods, not liking to take action until they are very sure it would be wise to do so.

There's proneness to overwork which can result in nervous tension and may cause problems with the digestion or the skin. Mars-Virgoans have to learn not to be such strict taskmasters, both with themselves and with others as well, of whom they can have too-high expectations.

MARS IN LIBRA

There's a certain amount of difficulty with energy flow here, a conflict between urge for action and a sense of inertia. Libra does, however, help to soften the aggressive and self-centered qualities associated with Mars. There is strong concern with justice and fairness, these people feeling outraged by injustice being perpetrated.

Those with Mars here often feel a need for a stable and permanent love relationship, with the feeling of completeness it brings for them. But some may have a tendency to fall in love too quickly and easily!

MARS IN SCORPIO

Here's someone with a tremendous emotional level and powerful desires, including a strong sex drive. A high level of intensity within the personality gives the potential to accomplish quite a lot, including goals that lesser mortals find too daunting. These people can be amazingly fearless, willing to fight uncompromisingly for their beliefs – this position of Mars is one for the true soldier.

If these Scorpio-Martians ever feel they have been scorned or thwarted, watch out, as intense jealousy and/or revenge can be a notable result.

MARS IN SAGITTARIUS

There's generally lots of enthusiasm in those with Mars here. This is often the sign of the 'crusader', the individual who fights to put across reforming ideas and tries earnestly to convert others. The ideas and opinions of those with Mars in this sign can be unconventional, maybe surprising, and some may incline to exaggerate. A love of the outdoors and of physical exercise is likely, plus desire for adventure and for foreign travel.

MARS IN CAPRICORN

Here, energy is put into achievement of ambitions. There's strong desire for success, and they have talent for clever calculation and organization in order to attain it. There may be danger of getting so wrapped up in acclaim that home life and love life suffer, so care needs to be taken lest they find themselves all alone when the bright lights fade.

Pride in doing a job well is a strong trait, and energies are carefully and gainfully employed. No frittering away of resources here!

MARS IN AQUARIUS

There is desire for independence and freedom in those with this combination. They're prone to sudden impulses and may seem unpredictable to friends and associates, and this can sometimes be troublesome. They are willful and insist on doing things their own way, often having to learn from their own mistakes!

In many, there is urge to reform or overthrow stuffy and

outdated forms of authority and replace them with something more enlightened and modern.

MARS IN PISCES

Energy flow may be dampened somewhat. There can be a certain lack of strength, with occasional need to retreat into quiet solitude in order to 'recharge the batteries'. Emotions and sentiment run high. Difficulty taking decisive action may cause problems due to energy being lost amid emotional stress.

This is a good position for working in hospitals or other caring professions, as there's a drive to help others combined with genuine desire to relieve suffering.

JUPITER SIGNS

JUPITER IN ARIES

Here we find someone with a positive desire to take action in attaining personal growth and mental expansion. This, like Mars in Sagittarius, can be a crusading combination: they have a pioneering spirit and a wish to reform. Generosity and an enthusiastic attitude will be notable. The need for self-betterment suggests that higher education may be particularly beneficial for them.

A tendency to take financial risks is likely – they need to ensure they take a realistic view of 'get rich quick' schemes and the like.

JUPITER IN TAURUS

This gives desire for good old-fashioned self-indulgent luxury. Gourmet food and comfortable surroundings are of tremendous appeal to Jupiter-Taureans, and they like to earn as much wealth as possible in order to provide these.

They're usually good-hearted, happy to share their fortune with others, although challenging aspects to Jupiter may bring health problems through excessive indulgence, so these individuals need to try to keep such Nero-like tendencies under reasonable control! Business ability is usually good, with patience and staying-power.

JUPITER IN GEMINI

Jupiter here gives desire for self-expansion through mental development. There's usually good working knowledge of many and varied subjects, the person being a bit of a 'know-it-all' (but usually in a nice way unless aspects are especially challenging!). Mental restlessness runs rampant and as is the case with most combinations involving Gemini, boredom comes easily.

Travel is of big appeal and many with Jupiter in Gemini have jobs that involve travelling. Interests may be scattered, and they may change their minds often. Teaching or writing ability are possible.

JUPITER IN CANCER

Unless there are challenging aspects to Jupiter, there will usually have been a happy family background behind them, in turn leading to the ability to provide a happy home for their own spouse and children. Generally there is much love between this person and their parents, especially the mother.

Jupiter-Cancerians are kind and generous to family and friends alike (often, friends are considered part of the family). Their parents may help them out financially.

JUPITER IN LEO

Here, self-betterment and expansion are taken on with confidence. These people have a taste for dramatic clothes and style and want to be admired for their appearance. They like to do things on a grand scale.

There is usually a strong constitution and plenty of enthusiasm, especially for anything that will make them look important! Love of children is a strong trait, and Jupiter-Leonians can be teachers or work with children.

JUPITER IN VIRGO

Here there may be conflict between the Jupiterian expansiveness and the Virgoan tendency to place emphasis upon small detail. They are generally good conscientious workers, with integrity and technical ability. With good aspects to Jupiter, they are likely to enjoy pleasant working conditions and workmates; if Jupiter aspects are challenging, there may be a more lazy attitude and a tendency to drift from one job to another.

Religious and moral beliefs are usually of a traditional type. Jupiter here is in a good place for those in the medical or other caring professions.

JUPITER IN LIBRA

Expansion in life is likely to come through partnership; these people are sociable and likeable, needing companionship and disliking being alone. Ideas on education, philosophy and religion tend to be influenced by their friends. Good taste, artistic ability and idealism are probable traits.

There may be too much of a tendency to try to be 'all things to all people' and to promise more than can actually be delivered, in order to gain the approval of others. There is a strong dislike for injustice.

JUPITER IN SCORPIO

The attributes associated with Jupiter take on a specially intense quality with Jupiter here. There is passion for life, with courage and magnetism, and interest in developing themselves through personal growth.

Emotions run deep, and perseverance, willpower and determination are usually notable. Jupiter-Scorpions can be passionate and uncompromising about their religious and spiritual beliefs.

JUPITER IN SAGITTARIUS

In its own sign, Jupiter's qualities are extra emphasized.

There is usually love of serious subjects, philosophy and foreign cultures; many have an urge to travel abroad, and experiences while doing so are generally beneficial. Residence in a foreign country may prove beneficial.

Jupiter-Sagittarians enjoy study for its own sake, and their outlook is philosophical and optimistic (unless aspects to Jupiter are very challenging). There is just about always affection for animals, horses being a particular favorite.

JUPITER IN CAPRICORN

The expansive principles of Jupiter are somewhat contracted by the restrictive forces of Saturn, Capricorn's ruler: self-control and a strong sense of responsibility may add a seemingly cheerless and rigid streak. But there's usually capacity for hard work and careful planning, often resulting in success.

A desire for recognition can spur them on to do great things, and most can carry responsibility well. Their attitude towards religious/moral values is usually conservative.

JUPITER IN AQUARIUS

Those with Jupiter here often show 'live and let live' principles – unbigoted and broadminded, they realize everyone has their own life to lead. They realize that tolerance and co-operation are necessary attributes in an imperfect world.

There may be attraction to causes that help to improve social conditions. Most people with Jupiter in Aquarius have a lot of friends and enjoy joining social groups.

JUPITER IN PISCES

This can give depth of compassion and understanding of others' needs. There's true desire to help those less fortunate. Capable of self-sacrifice, these people can identify with the suffering of others and will go to great lengths to assist.

A friendly personality coupled with an aura of benevolence makes them well-liked; they have to take care, however, not to be fooled easily by fabricated hard-luck stories. Many find they need to get away from it all from time to time in order to renew their spirits and restore themselves.

SATURN SIGNS

SATURN IN ARIES

These individuals may alternate between periods of strength and inertia; desire to take action is sometimes curbed by conditions beyond their control. There's ingenuity and ability to accomplish much, although maybe with some hindrance along the way.

Persistence and independence are usually strong traits. They are reasoned and cautious when arguing a point.

SATURN IN TAURUS

These individuals are likely to seek out (especially after their late twenties) stable, lucrative careers and home lives. They are usually practical and reliable. Careful with money, they're the ones who like to put something by for a rainy day.

Patience and endurance are strong. If there are challenging aspects to Saturn, they may be overly obsessed with material possessions.

SATURN IN GEMINI

This combination helps to exert a steadying and practical influence on the mind. There's mental versatility and ability to think logically. There may have been illness or other hardship early in life if aspects are challenging; these problems tend to improve as they grow older.

Their attitude towards most things is skeptical, always wanting to see good scientific proof for everything.

SATURN IN CANCER

Those with Saturn here need a steady and reliable home life. They take their domestic responsibilities seriously, maybe to the point of seeming a dampening influence upon the home scene; a more light-hearted outlook could be helpful.

Some may find it hard to express their feelings openly. Desire to own one's own home is strong, and they will plan carefully to try to make that happen.

SATURN IN LEO

Here the ambition identified with Saturn combines with the need for admiration and recognition represented by Leo – a formidable combination!

There's compulsion for leadership and authority, and a wish to be considered important. (some with challenging Saturn aspects need to guard against ending up becoming a tyrant!). Sometimes inability to recognize other peoples' limitations causes problems.

SATURN IN VIRGO

Those with Saturn here can exhibit real devotion to duty; some are downright workaholics. There can be a tendency towards expecting too high a standard of work, behavior, etc. from others who are only human.

Obsession with minuscule details can obscure the overall picture ('unable to see the woods for the trees'), but their talent for precision suits them well for work that demands exactitude, such as medical research, computer technology, or scientific labwork.

SATURN IN LIBRA

This is the best position for Saturn, its severeness and restrictiveness softened by the gentle Venusian qualities of Libra. These people generally have good judgment, are just and fair, and have a kind and pleasant aura.

There's good planning ability, and they are flexible and reasonable in dealing with others. Those with Saturn here may marry later in life than most, or marry someone of a specially serious, mature, responsible type.

SATURN IN SCORPIO

These individuals are sometimes found shouldering burdens with serious intensity – those who 'have a cross to bear'. They can feel put-upon, can be secretive and brood.

They're usually ambitious for success, pursuing it with persistence and determination. They are serious and thoughtful about most things, and if there are challenging aspects to Saturn there may be deep, powerful emotions about something that for some reason needs to be kept hidden or secret.

SATURN IN SAGITTARIUS

These people are very serious in their pursuit of knowledge, and some become involved in philosophy and religion. They're able to keep to long-term study and assimilate most of what they learn. Honest and direct, many project an air of dignity.

Sometimes there's conflict between the wish to expand (Sagittarius) and the need for caution (Saturn), so that others may think of these people as self-contradictory at times.

SATURN IN CAPRICORN

In its own sign, Saturn brings especially strong ambition and desire for worldly success. Patience and self-discipline are in evidence, and personal sacrifice may be made for the sake of ambitions. There is a need to achieve, to make something of oneself, to get somewhere in life.

They often like to be in a position of authority. With challenging Saturn aspects, some may be somewhat selfish, or have an unfortunate tendency to wallow in misery of their own making.

SATURN IN AQUARIUS

This combination can give an original mind with scientific leanings. There's a sense of responsibility towards friends and social groups, and strong principles. Ability to plan and work for the benefit of others is strong.

There can be a formal, intellectual aura about some of these people, a sort of professorial type of demeanor – they may actually be professors by profession, or at least give off that sort of vibe!

SATURN IN PISCES

This is a good combination for those who display some psychic interest or talent, as Saturn here can give a practical attitude towards these interests and the ability to use them wisely. By the same token, it's also a helpful combination for those in the caring professions.

On the other hand, with challenging aspects to Saturn in Pisces, some may be moody and overly-sensitive, maybe with a degree of phobia or anxiety. In any case, there is compassion and self-sacrifice, and many are suited for work in large institutions that deal with helping others.

URANUS, NEPTUNE AND PLUTO SIGNS

The three outer planets move so slowly that everyone born within a certain span of years will have any one of them in the same sign as the other people of that age group; they are therefore known as generational influence planets.

Staying in the same sign for so many years at a time (Uranus about 7 years, Neptune about 13 and Pluto varying from about 12 to about 32) the sign position of these planets affect an individual's chart not in a personal way but more as a representation of the generation as a whole.

As a result, descriptions of the sign positions of those planets won't be covered in this book, which is meant to be a brief and simplified guide aimed at beginners. You can get hold of more advanced books if you do want to go into further detail.

Their appearances through the Houses do affect the individual in a specific way, though, and these will be covered in the section 'Planets in the Houses'.

THE ASCENDANT AND THE MIDHEAVEN

THE ASCENDANT

ARIES RISING

This rising sign strengthens the whole chart. These people are generally robust, energetic, daring and assertive. The tone of the rest of chart will tell how strong these traits are and how wisely they're used, but in any case there's usually strength of spirit and body. They are impulsive, fast-acting, fast-speaking and fast-thinking. Not liking to waste time, they can make quick, spur-of-the-moment decisions.

Taurus on the second House cusp helps give a practical attitude towards money, something anyone with a strong Arian streak needs! Ambition coupled with fondness for money can spur many of these people on to become quite successful.

Libra on seventh House cusp suggests that the best marriage partner for our Aries Rising person would be someone possessing the traits normally associated with the sign of Libra: someone calm, harmony-loving, capable of keeping the peace, able to deal tactfully with all situations. He/she would be charming, maybe artistic or musical, and nice to look at.

Capricorn on tenth House cusp gives enthusiastic pursuit of recognition; they spare no effort in their fight to make it to the top, though sometimes stepping on a few toes along the way!

TAURUS RISING

They are generally easy-going, enjoying peace and contentment and comfort. There's fondness for good food and drink. Many have deep love of the countryside and seek to own their own plot of land, to be 'close to the earth'. Failing this, they will at least be happy to potter in their garden (or someone else's). Many have musical ability, especially for singing, and they are often attractive in an earthy, sensual way, with large, pretty, cow-like eyes!

Gemini on second House cusp shows that they are capable of coming up with inventive ways of making money. Some may earn from more than one source.

With Scorpio on the seventh House cusp, we find their ideal partner to be someone with the sort of traits typified by the sign of Scorpio: someone strong-willed, magnetic and dynamic, an intense and passionate type. Many with this Rising sign marry early in life, and some may rush into marriage too hastily. Life may change for the better after marriage, especially if there are good aspects to Venus or any planets in the seventh.

Aquarius on the tenth House cusp helps them to bring originality and ingenuity into the profession, and the career may be out of the ordinary in some way.

GEMINI RISING

These people are endowed with mental energy. They love to read, talk, and think, all of which they do constantly (often all at the same). They are versatile and original in their ideas, good at keeping up a conversation and keeping others interested. Restless and curious, they get out a lot and like to travel just for the change of scenery. Overall, there's a need for communication, whether it be through speech, writing, or action. Many great writers, especially of the witty variety (e.g., George Bernard Shaw) have had this Ascendant. They retain a youthful image and appearance well into old age, and stay popular with those of younger age groups.

Cancer on second House cusp suggests that their financial situations may be bound up with the emotions in some way. They may be the sort who go out on spending sprees when depressed and feel much better afterward, or they may earn money in matters to do with others' emotional states, such as through therapy, psychology, or leisure interests.

Sagittarius on seventh House cusp indicates that an ideal partner would be someone of a Sagittarian type: he/she would be adventure-loving, optimistic and philosophical, with a good sense of humor, easygoing, enjoying education and travel.

Pisces on the tenth gives idealism about the career. An artistic, showbiz, or medical career are possibilities.

CANCER RISING

These people are emotional, moody and sensitive. They're kind and protective with a true 'motherly' instinct. Sometimes they can be hard to fathom, as they are subject to extreme changes of mood; they can be all smiles one minute and all crabby the next. Many of their problems stem from being too receptive to others' emotions and moods. They need to learn to take a more detached view and to try not to worry about every little thing – often easier said than done, but relaxation techniques, meditation and the like can be a great help.

Leo on the second House cusp indicates that money may

be made attaining a position of authority or some sort of leadership. There's a good deal of pride and ego involved in their financial prowess.

Capricorn on seventh House cusp shows that the ideal romantic partner would be someone possessing traits associated with the sign of Capricorn: someone practical, cautious, stable, reliable, with a good ironic sense of humor and an urge to advance in life. They are cautious about selecting a marriage partner, and may marry later in life than most.

Aries on the tenth House cusp shows ambition and assertiveness in the career. There is a keen sense of competition and attraction to a career that demands vigor and an ability to keep on one's toes.

LEO RISING

There's a dignified, dramatic, kingly aura about them. They make a commanding presence, exuding warmth and affection, and demanding nothing but your undying admiration end attention in return. They love to be noticed and to show off in order to stand out from the crowd. Many present a striking appearance and they often have flowing manes of hair that do give them a lion-like look. The arts and theatre are of appeal, and they may have talent for the performing arts themselves.

Virgo on second House cusp helps give a careful, precise attitude towards finances, therefore suiting them well for work to do with accounting, banking and the like. Earnings may also come through writing or other forms of communication.

With Leo Rising, the sign on the seventh House cusp is Aquarius, which shows an attraction for romantic partners of an Aquarian type: someone original, independent, ingenious, unconventional and maybe scientifically-minded. The marriage relationship may be unusual in some way.

Taurus on the tenth shows an attraction towards a profession involving art or other forms of beauty, or anything that brings pleasure to others.

VIRGO RISING

Those with Virgo rising are perfectionists and have a love of good quality and craftsmanship. Intellectually inclined, they like to keep their minds busy, and they enjoy study and research. They need order and efficiency – being thrust into a chaotic environment makes them disorientated and uncomfortable. They enjoy reading and assimilating facts, carefully analyzing and sifting them, mentally storing them for future use. Often there is an interest in nutrition and in healthcare in general.

Libra on second House cusp suggests that the best financial progress may be made working with a partner. There may be desire or ability to earn money through artistic activities. In any case, much of the money earned will be spent on things of beauty.

Pisces on the seventh House cusp indicates that the ideal romantic partner will be of a type associated with the sign of Pisces: someone who is romantic, caring, gentle, kind, compassionate, maybe a little dreamy and artistic, and with a good sense of humor.

Gemini on the tenth House cusp shows attraction towards a profession to do with communication or travel, and the need for a mentally stimulating and varied career.

LIBRA RISING

These individuals are usually graceful and attractive in appearance, with refined features and tasteful, maybe elegant, attire. They are charmers and tactful and just about always popular. There is generally a sense of justice and fairness, and a striving for peace and harmony. Most are fond of the arts, music, anything beautiful, and could be talented in those areas as well.

Scorpio on the second House cusp gives intensity to the earning of money. Some will have talent for transforming a previously failing or unprofitable business venture into something really lucrative, or regenerating junk into items of value.

Aries on seventh House cusp shows that the ideal romantic partner may be someone with Aries-like traits: someone daring, assertive, enthusiastic, energetic, robust of constitution, willing and able to tackle and overcome obstacles.

Cancer on the tenth suggests professional pursuits that have to do with the domestic side of things, or that appeal to the emotions somehow, and may involve women's interests in particular.

SCORPIO RISING

These individuals have a magnetic, intense quality about them that can be irresistible, almost mesmerizing. There's often something remarkable about their eyes: a vivid color, a penetrating gaze. They are capable of near-superhuman persistence and determination; once they've set their minds on something of importance to them, they will literally go through hell to attain it. Halfway measures do not satisfy them; there is a real all or nothing attitude. They don't take anything lightly, whether it concerns love, work, play, anything.

Sagittarius on the second House cusp generally indicates that financially, they think on a grand scale and take risks that most others wouldn't. They are persistent and confident and good at getting the job done.

Taurus on seventh House cusp shows that a good romantic partner would be a Taurean type: someone capable and no-nonsense, practical, reliable, affectionate, down-to-earth, security-providing, probably an art or music lover.

Leo on tenth shows that much pride is wrapped up in their professional abilities. There is desire to be a leader in one's field and to receive the relevant admiration for it.

SAGITTARIUS RISING

Those with this Rising sign set themselves high goals, not resting until these have been achieved – and then, they find yet higher goals to aim for, and go off in pursuit of those. They're friendly, good-humored and philosophical; some are happy-go-lucky to the point of recklessness. Personal freedom is of great importance; these Centaurs like to be able to just pack up and run off whenever the mood strikes them. Often, they find it hard to settle down to a conventional lifestyle. Many have a deep love of nature that borders on the spiritual - long walks in the countryside or an afternoon at a secluded beach fill them with joy and awe. Love of animals is often a strong trait.

Capricorn on second House cusp helps gives a practical and responsible attitude towards finances (although if there are challenging aspects in the chart, caution about money may be carried to the extent of miserliness).

Gemini on seventh House cusp shows that the ideal romantic partner is likely to be one possessing the traits associated with the sign Gemini: someone intelligent, intellectual, versatile, eternally youthful, talkative, well-informed and able to keep them interested. There may be more than one marriage or significant love relationship.

Virgo on the tenth House cusp shows that this individual is organized and efficient in the course of duty. Their reputations are important to them; they are careful to project the 'right' sort of image. The profession may deal with communication or with health (or both).

CAPRICORN RISING

Those with this sign rising often give an impression of reserve and aloofness. People may think of them as stand-offish, even snobbish, but in reality most of these Goats are either just plain shy or else brooding with melancholy over how unfairly life seems to treat them. They're serious and intent; they tend to be 'old when young', maybe even to the point of going prematurely grey. An intrinsic insecurity drives them to try to better themselves and to accomplish things - they feel a need to do something important with their lives. But as the years go on, especially after the 28th year, they begin to feel more at ease with themselves and with the world at large.

Aquarius on second House cusp shows ability to come up with new and unconventional ways of making money. Earnings may come from completely unexpected sources. Independence is needed at their jobs, and many are happiest working freelance.

Cancer on seventh House cusp shows that the ideal romantic partner is likely to be someone of a Cancerian type:

someone sensitive, protective, home-loving, imaginative and intuitive. There is usually a strong bond between the two partners.

Libra on tenth House cusp gives ability for work involving co-operation with others, using tact and diplomacy. Some may advance in their professions simply by being charming to those in authority!

AQUARIUS RISING

Those with this ascendant are often unique in thought and behavior and even in appearance as well: many are much taller than average, and they may be striking-looking in some way or other. Inventive and forward looking, they are the ones who get referred to as 'ahead of their time'. Their unpredictability may seem bewildering to some, but they are rarely dull! There are geniuses to be found among them, and many do well in fields to do with maths, computers, or science.

Pisces on second House cusp could make some a little impractical when it comes to money matters. However, they mean well and often put money into worthwhile causes. Earnings may come through unusual, original ideas.

Leo on seventh House cusp shows that they would be best suited by a romantic partner with attributes of a type associated with the sign Leo: someone who is warm, generous, outgoing, outstanding, powerful, dramatic and capable.

Scorpio on tenth House cusp shows much intensity, power and charisma poured into the profession, and these people may be able to win others over through sheer irresistible magnetism.

PISCES RISING

Those with Pisces ascendant are idealistic, imaginative, possessing high intuition and vision. In appearance, they can seem unworldly: mysterious, ethereal, dreamy, often with large doe-like eyes with a faraway look to them. They are kind and gentle, with much sympathy and compassion, and those who get to know them can end up adoring them. Sometimes they get into trouble by seeing others as nicer than they really are; they overlook, or make unrealistic and idealistic allowances for, negative traits and downright nastiness, which can leave themselves vulnerable to being taken advantage of.

Aries on second House cusp shows that earnings may come about through starting new enterprises and projects. Much energy and resourcefulness is put into the earning of the weekly wage. They may make impulsive purchases.

Virgo on the seventh House cusp indicates that someone of a Virgoan type may be an ideal romantic partner: someone efficient, well-organized, hard-working, perfectionist, practical, with a caring and nurturing attitude.

Sagittarius on tenth House cusp may bring success in fields to do with travel, education, law or religion, and these individuals are usually fortunate in their business dealings.

THE MIDHEAVEN

ARIES MIDHEAVEN

Others see these people as robust, energetic and assertive. There is ability to inspire enthusiasm, and to make others think this individual is brave, daring and a good leader.

They can succeed at work through sheer brashness, swaying others with their aura of self-confidence.

TAURUS MIDHEAVEN

They're seen by others as warm-hearted, affectionate, pleasure-loving, stable and reliable. They will often be the sort that people come to with their problems because they know they'll get a 'there, there' and much comforting reassurance.

If the rest of the chart agrees, they may follow a career (or active hobby) to do with art or music.

GEMINI MIDHEAVEN

These people are seen as chatty, informative, a gold mine of information on every imaginable subject. They appear restless and tense a lot of the time: the proverbial sufferers of 'itchy feet' and 'ants in the pants'.

Quick and witty in speech, they feel their status with others depends on their ability to communicate interestingly and effectively.

CANCER MIDHEAVEN

This Midheaven sign gives its owner the aura of concern for others, of possessing a protective attitude.

They may be seen as moody and unpredictable, others not being sure whether they will be sympathized with or snapped at. But when in a good mood, they are always ready to lend an ear and give kindly advice.

LEO MIDHEAVEN

They have an aura of capability and authority that inspires confidence in others (that is, as long as the rest of the chart agrees; otherwise they may give the impression of these abilities but with no real strength behind it!).

They generally like to show off, whether by becoming involved in the performing arts, or just by dressing loudly and being brash – they are the proverbial 'guy who ends up with the lampshade on his head at parties'!

VIRGO MIDHEAVEN

These individuals often give the outward impression of being prim and proper, but don't let that fool you. Underneath that reserved exterior, often lurks all manner of interesting ideas.

They are usually seen to be efficient and well-organized in their work and neat in their appearance.

LIBRA MIDHEAVEN

They are often cast in the role of peacemaker as they tend to appear so tactful, diplomatic, co-operative and harmonious. People often seek out their company simply because they give off such a friendly, sociable demeanor.

They are often graceful and refined in appearance, and usually nice to look at as well.

SCORPIO MIDHEAVEN

These people give off an intense, magnetic sort of quality. They may project a dark, brooding aura, and may seem secretive, a real 'Man (or Woman) of Mystery'. They're people who like to keep a low profile.

They are seen as able to approach tasks in a determined, single-minded and passionate way that can seem almost scary.

SAGITTARIUS MIDHEAVEN

Those with their Midheaven in this sign are generally seen as honest and straightforward. Independence and freedom-loving traits are in evidence, along with fondness for adventure.

They're seen as always flitting off to some interesting place or another. Their outlook appears easy-going and philosophical

CAPRICORN MIDHEAVEN

People will tend to see them as practical, reliable, down-to-earth types. They display a notable sense of ambition – maybe a little too much for the comfort of some (especially their bosses).

They're often seen as embarking on one project or another in which they endeavor to better themselves materially or spiritually or both.

AQUARIUS MIDHEAVEN

Seen as original in thought and action, they're innovative, unconventional and exciting to be around. Other people may be astounded by their ability to expound on all sorts of fascinating scientific and mathematical facts.

They're outspoken and often say unexpected things that take others by surprise.

PISCES MIDHEAVEN

They are seen as gentle and kind, maybe dreamy and romantic, always caring and sensitive. There's a vulnerable quality that makes others want to protect and take care of them.

People enjoy their company because they are receptive and sympathetic and usually have a good sense of humor.

PLANETS IN THE HOUSES

THE SUN

SUN IN FIRST HOUSE

Usually bestows good health and strong constitution unless there are very challenging aspects to it. These people are very self-aware; if carried to extremes, they could be a little too self-centered. Opinions are strong and not easily influenced by others.

SUN IN SECOND HOUSE

Financial matters take on particularly strong importance for them. There's usually notable desire for financial independence. Many with the Sun in the 2nd House try to accumulate as much wealth as possible.

SUN IN THIRD HOUSE

There's a powerful need to communicate – there may be writing talent. School life will usually have been enjoyed (unless there are challenging aspects to the contrary in the chart) and some may have won distinction. Brothers, sisters and neighbors are especially important to these individuals.

SUN IN FOURTH HOUSE

Desire for a nice House and a happy and secure domestic life typifies those with the Sun in this House. They like to make their home a place of beauty and comfort, and enjoy entertaining at home. There's usually a strong wish to own their own home and make it a very appealing haven, their own castle.

SUN IN FIFTH HOUSE

Here we find an individual with an intrinsic urge to create. Many people talented in the arts, especially the performing arts, will have their Sun here. There's zest for life, and they express themselves in a forceful and dramatic way. Love affairs are also of great importance to them.

SUN IN SIXTH HOUSE

These people are usually hardworking, taking pride in their work and seeking recognition for it. The work may bring them before the public eye. Work may be to do with health or with being of service to others in some way. Good aspects to the Sun help strengthen the health, while challenging aspects may weaken it and possibly require a special diet or other health regimen to be followed.

SUN IN SEVENTH HOUSE

If free of challenging aspects, the Sun here can indicate a happy marriage. A permanent love relationship is of particularly high importance to them – for some, it can be the most important thing. General success in life may improve after marriage. Partnerships of all sorts, both in business and pleasure, are specially beneficial.

SUN IN EIGHTH HOUSE

Interest in the psychic and mystical, or in any case the mysteries of life in general, are likely. There may be involvement with the finances of others and, if there are good aspects, there may be the possibility of inheritance for themselves.

SUN IN NINTH HOUSE

Love of foreign travel is prominent here, and this is an excellent indication of those who will travel extensively abroad or emigrate. Higher education may appeal greatly, as may subjects to do with philosophy, religion or law. Life might revolve around travel or foreign matters.

SUN IN TENTH HOUSE

With the Sun in this House, we often find the type of person for whom the career is the most important thing in life. They throw themselves into their work, and the profession often brings them into the public eye. There may be a sense of a 'calling' for the profession. Many have a deep-rooted need for fame.

SUN IN ELEVENTH HOUSE

Those with the Sun here place great importance on

friendships and group activities. They may benefit from the help of friends in high places. There can be leadership amongst their social circle, and a liking for organizing social functions. Involvement in organizations that help society may be a notable and noble tendency.

SUN IN TWELFTH HOUSE

With this position, the energy of the Sun is turned inward. There may be much soul-searching, the individual tending to be on the introverted side and maybe a little shy. There may be a need to withdraw from social activity from time to time in order to regain peace of mind from quiet solitude. The mind is sensitive and in tune with the subconscious – in some, there may seem to be telepathic abilities. A desire to help others may be a strong point.

THE MOON

MOON IN FIRST HOUSE

These people are greatly influenced by things that affect them emotionally. They are impressionable, moody and changeable, many of their attitudes being influenced by those of others. A specially strong bond with their mother is common. Many with the Moon here have round, full faces and/or a fleshy physique.

MOON IN SECOND HOUSE

There's pronounced emotional need for financial security among those with the Moon here; they feel that a lot of money is necessary in order to ensure a happy and secure home. The financial situation may be noticeably on the changeable side, with income running the gamut from lean times to fruitful and back again.

MOON IN THIRD HOUSE

They may be changeable in ideas and opinions. Early childhood conditioning and family opinion stay with them and color their attitudes in later life. There may be stronger than usual bonds with brothers, sisters and neighbors, neighbors often being considered part of the family. Restlessness and enjoyment of short journeys are likely.

MOON IN FOURTH HOUSE

A good deal of maternal/paternal instinct usually emerges in those with the Moon here. Family matters are of much importance, and they feel they can't be happy unless their domestic lives are positive and secure. They may be greatly influenced by their parents, especially their mother. An interest in history and/or family ancestry is likely.

MOON IN FIFTH HOUSE

There can be changeable emotions in love affairs, and they may also tend to depend on their partner a lot. They are romantic and are imaginative in their ways of showing affection. Creativity in artistic fields is likely, especially to do with fine arts, dance, anything that can be romantic and dreamy. Love of children is strong, and this placing of the Moon often indicates they will have several children.

MOON IN SIXTH HOUSE

Their state of health can be strongly influenced by their emotions. With challenging aspects there could be psychosomatically-induced illnesses. Health may have been weak in childhood – sometimes there's need for a special diet or other regimen in order to stay fit. Attraction to work in fields to do with health or science is possible. Their ability to do their job well can depend on their emotional state on the day.

MOON IN SEVENTH HOUSE

There's strong need for emotional security and they marry for love rather than for more material considerations. They feel a lack of fulfillment in life unless they have a happy emotional relationship. The marriage partner may be of a moody type. Business partnerships with women may be particularly beneficial.

MOON IN EIGHTH HOUSE

A deeply emotional need to dig into the mysteries of life is often found here – there's often interest in the psychic sciences as well. There may be involvement with public finance, and possibly inheritance through a female relative or acquaintance.

MOON IN NINTH HOUSE

Here the Moon gives a real love of travel and a probability of taking up residence abroad or at least somewhere far from the place of birth. These individuals are likely to be interested in serious subjects (such as law, philosophy, religion, foreign languages or cultures, history) and able to study well. Some may have a strong emotional attachment to their religion.

MOON IN TENTH HOUSE

These people have a strong emotional desire for recognition and may well be brought before the public eye in matters to do with their profession. There may be several career changes along the way. The career may be helped along more so by women than by men. If fame is achieved there may be little time allowed for private life. Some have family who were ambitious for their success and helped to spur them on.

MOON IN ELEVENTH HOUSE

Here we find someone with a need to be surrounded by friends much of the time, and to be actively involved in group activities. Acquaintances are many and varied, and often of help: 'a friend in need'. A larger proportion of their friends are likely to be female. Their aims and objectives in life may be inconsistent, varying with their changes of mood or circumstances.

MOON IN TWELFTH HOUSE

Those with the Moon here enjoy solitude and need to get away from the rat-race as often as possible in order to restore their easily shattered sensitivities. The imagination and intuition are powerful and should be developed and given a good positive outlet. They may be a little shy and easily hurt.

MERCURY

MERCURY IN FIRST HOUSE

There's special emphasis on the intellect in those with Mercury here. Lots of mental energy is indicated, with a need for intellectual stimulation and challenge. They are talkative and enjoy writing, needing to communicate with others as often, and at as great a length, as possible. Restlessness and a desire to get out and about are very strong traits. Generally, the intelligence is high and the wit quick.

MERCURY IN SECOND HOUSE

Earning money through sales work or as some sort of rep – something requiring the gift of the gab in order to make money – could be rewarding. They may find clever ways of making money, and many of these people work in businesses to do with communication. They're usually good at quick financial decisions.

MERCURY IN THIRD HOUSE

Intellectual ability is notable, and they probably did well in school. They can be good writers and speakers and are usually pretty talkative in general. A lot of their time may be spent in short distance travel and in writing letters. Learning as much as possible is of huge appeal for them.

MERCURY IN FOURTH HOUSE

There's a strong probability of mental activity carried out at home, such as study or working from there. They may have a large home library and enjoy making good use of it. Frequent changes of residence are common; some may even prefer a nomadic existence.

MERCURY IN FIFTH HOUSE

Creative powers of an intellectual nature are likely. These people can be inventive writers, teachers, art critics and the like. They enjoy games of mental competition. There may be many love affairs and most of these individuals are attracted to those of an intellectual type. Some of those with Mercury here have no children but rather 'give birth to' works of art or literature.

MERCURY IN SIXTH HOUSE

They're often the ones who really throw themselves mentally into their work, striving to amass as much skill and knowledge as possible in order to make their labors more effective. They like to keep up with the latest developments in their field. A perfectionist streak and an inclination to overwork may bring digestive upsets.

MERCURY IN SEVENTH HOUSE

They prefer working in partnership rather than going it alone. Talent for communicating with the public is likely. In both in love and in business, they prefer someone mentally stimulating with whom they feel intellectual rapport. Their ideal partner would be witty and quick-thinking, and/or a lot younger.

MERCURY IN EIGHTH HOUSE

They have a great curiosity about the mysterious side of life, maybe including the psychic and occult. They can be secretive, enjoying intrigue and clandestine plan-making. Mystery stories are likely to appeal, and some may work in a profession dealing with crime.

MERCURY IN NINTH HOUSE

There's attraction to higher learning and acquisition of degrees and other written proofs of cerebral accomplishment. There will be curiosity about other countries and cultures. They're keen on travel and will go a long way to satisfy their curiosity and to gain knowledge that they feel will be of importance.

MERCURY IN TENTH HOUSE

These people want to learn as much as they can to further their careers. There's usually good ability to communicate with those in positions of power who can help them. Their careers have to be especially varied and mentally stimulating, or else they go out of their minds with boredom. A career to do with communication, travel, the media, is most likely to appeal.

MERCURY IN ELEVENTH HOUSE

Those with Mercury here actively seek out friends and social groups with whom they can exchange inspiring ideas and opinions. They like to both teach, and learn from, their acquaintances. They're likely to have many friends, a lot of whom may be of a much younger age group. Social life will probably be very lively.

MERCURY IN TWELFTH HOUSE

Here we may find someone who lives much in the past – 'just me and my memories'. Ideas are strongly colored by past experiences and conditioning. Some may be secretive about their opinions, a bit shy of letting others know what they really think. There's a liking for working in seclusion. Intuition and imagination are usually strong.

VENUS

VENUS IN FIRST HOUSE

Venus here usually bestows grace, a pleasant personality, charm and attractive looks; it's especially good at enhancing the beauty of women. There's a love of beautiful clothes and of making oneself look attractive. Many of those with Venus here have a degree of luck running through their lives and could, if there are challenging aspects to Venus, become somewhat lazy and spoiled as a result!

VENUS IN SECOND HOUSE

Importance is placed on acquisition of beautiful and expensive possessions. There's a strong emphasis on earning as much as possible (or seeking well-off romantic partners!) in order to fulfill this urge. Some may earn money through the arts or music, and many spend their earnings as quickly as they come in.

VENUS IN THIRD HOUSE

Love of literature and the fine arts is likely. They're fluent and graceful talkers who communicate in a harmonious manner. Short-distance travel is undertaken often and they enjoy it as much for the pleasure of the journey as for actually getting there. Relationships with siblings and neighbors are likely to be especially good. These people are often able to express themselves poetically and romantically in writing – they may write romantic poems and love letters of eloquent beauty.

VENUS IN FOURTH HOUSE

These individuals love for their homes to be places of beauty and comfort. They enjoy entertaining friends and loved ones there, and are good at making people feel at home. They like to decorate their homes in an artistic manner and enjoy having flowers and potted plants scattered about. There's usually much love for, and closeness to, their parents.

VENUS IN FIFTH HOUSE

An almost exaggerated pleasure in love affairs, the arts, and/or sports exists in many with Venus here. Romance is all-important. There may be artistic talent, especially for the performing arts. They're affectionate and popular and generally are very attractive to the opposite sex, and there is usually a strong love of children.

VENUS IN SIXTH HOUSE

They often follow artistic careers or at least work in surroundings of beauty and harmony (or would like to do so). Social and romantic contacts may be made more so through their work environment than elsewhere. Relationships with workmates are friendly and enjoyable, and there is definite dislike of dirty work or hard physical labor. Their health will usually be good.

VENUS IN SEVENTH HOUSE

If there are no challenging aspects, Venus here is very often indicative of happy marriage. Marriage (or other long-term relationship) can bring especially great fulfillment to these people, and they marry for love and are able to show their affections freely (if, again, there are not overly nasty challenging aspects). Business partnerships are also likely to be beneficial.

VENUS IN EIGHTH HOUSE

This often indicates financial gain through marriage or an inheritance. Emotions are intense, and the person may be a little on the jealous side. Sex life is usually particularly harmonious if Venus is free of challenging aspects. An unchallenged Venus here also often indicates that this person will live to a comfortable and peaceful old age.

VENUS IN NINTH HOUSE

Attraction to long-distance travel is emphasized, and they may often take long trips for pleasure. Higher education is enjoyed, and they find university life happy and fulfilling. Many are well educated and of refined tastes. Often there is attraction to foreign people and lands, and some may marry someone of a different nationality and/or go to live abroad.

VENUS IN TENTH HOUSE

If free of challenging aspects, this often brings success and pleasure in the profession. The career may be to do with diplomacy, or the arts. Artists with Venus here stand a chance of actually earning good money for their efforts! Alternatively, they may marry someone who has a good career that brings wealth. There's usually success in business dealings with the opposite sex.

VENUS IN ELEVENTH HOUSE

These people tend to be popular and have many friends, and are especially good at maintaining warm, happy relationships. They do well in clubs and societies, able to be helpful and diplomatic, and make worthwhile friendships there. Many of the friends will be of the opposite sex and some will be of an artistic or musical nature.

VENUS IN TWELFTH HOUSE

Those with Venus here have a love of peace and solitude. The mind is emotional and artistic, and there can be much inspired activity. Some may be secretive about their love affairs – sometimes there could be a love relationship with someone who is married, or that needs to be kept secret for some other reason. These people are generally sensitive and retiring.

MARS

MARS IN FIRST HOUSE

They can have an almost ridiculous amount of energy, are aggressive and outgoing, impatient and impulsive. Mars here helps strengthen the health, and many are of a rugged type. Competitive drive is high and they have notable stamina. Accident-proneness is also likely, especially for cuts, burns and head injuries. If Mars is in a fire sign they may have red or reddish hair, and some men start losing hair at an early age.

MARS IN SECOND HOUSE

There's active desire to earn lots of money, and usually to spend lots of it as well. They may be impulsive about the way they both earn and spend. Many have a fierce desire to run their own business, and when they do they can be very competitive. Some with challenging aspects to Mars may be overly concerned with material things, maybe even to the point of stealing.

MARS IN THIRD HOUSE

These people probably were particularly keen at school, often highly competitive there. They will have fought to protect siblings and friends from bullies. Alternatively, with challenging aspects to Mars, they may have been bullies themselves! They're aggressive and assertive in communicating, and can jump to conclusions without thinking things out properly. A tendency to take short trips on impulse is likely.

MARS IN FOURTH HOUSE

They work vigorously to improve their homes and family life. Home hobbies requiring physical strength (DIY, keep-fit exercises, martial arts, etc.) are likely to be of appeal. If other areas of the chart don't contradict, these activities help them build a strong constitution that keeps them active into old age. Many take active interest in the environment and will work to support ecological causes.

MARS IN FIFTH HOUSE

A highly romantic sort who eagerly pursues the object of their affections is indicated here. Competitive sports appeal to them, and artists who work with sharp tools (sculptors, carvers, cutters of lino or woodcut prints) often have Mars here. Some may have accident-prone children.

MARS IN SIXTH HOUSE

Extraordinarily hardworking, quick and energetic, they expect the same from co-workers and subordinates which means, of course, that they may expect too much. These individuals have to be careful they don't burn themselves out through overwork. Work is often of a highly-skilled precise type, and they take pride in doing it well. Some may be argumentative with co-workers. They can suffer headaches, fevers and cuts, and/or tend to get injured at work.

MARS IN SEVENTH HOUSE

An active, lively attitude towards love relationships and marriage is held by these people. They're attracted to marriage partners who are also of an assertive and energetic type. If there are challenging aspects, they may tend to pick arguments with their partner. Many of those with Mars here are good at dealing with the public and can be good at sales or public relations.

MARS IN EIGHTH HOUSE

They may take a keen interest in the mysterious sides of life, such as unsolved mysteries, or in the occult. Interest in psychology, surgery, or investigation is common with Mars here. Desires and emotions are intense. There's a likelihood of active involvement in others' finances, and an aggressive attitude is taken towards these.

MARS IN NINTH HOUSE

This often indicates someone with a particularly strong liking for travel (especially abroad) and adventure. There may be active participation in causes of a philosophical, religious, or educational nature or to do with social welfare. If other areas of the chart agree, they could be good leaders in these areas. There's a general thirst for experience and for learning as much as possible.

MARS IN TENTH HOUSE

Desire for status is coupled with competitiveness, and no energy is spared in the fight to get to the top. They can make good leaders and managers, though some with challenging aspects could become drunk with power and too dictatorial – a 'little Hitler'. In that latter case, sometimes Mars here indicates someone who achieves notoriety rather than fame.

MARS IN ELEVENTH HOUSE

Energy and enthusiasm are thrown into social activity. Friends are likely to be of a lively, aggressive type. Many of these individuals make friends quickly but also lose friends equally quickly! Some can be good leaders, if maybe a little pushy. With very challenging aspects, they may be too argumentative with friends.

MARS IN TWELFTH HOUSE

They are capable of fighting to help those who are badly-off. The individual can be very secretive; work may be carried out in seclusion. They're prone to suppressed anger which may suddenly explode and stun the unfortunate bystander; it would be a good idea to channel these repressed energies into healthier outlets (a punching-bag, maybe).

JUPITER

JUPITER IN FIRST HOUSE

They are usually outgoing, friendly, benevolent, well-liked. The outlook is philosophical, and some may be of a spiritual or religious type. Love of higher education and adventure are likely. Some may tend to exaggerate things. They're often of a big, tall build, some becoming overweight in later years.

JUPITER IN SECOND HOUSE

This can be quite a fortunate influence. Many of these individuals are able to make money easily and have good financial luck all-round. However (especially with challenging aspects to Jupiter) money may disappear in a big way as well. They may be too extravagant or take too much for granted when undertaking financial or business ventures, not seeing the possible snags.

JUPITER IN THIRD HOUSE

They're likely to have enjoyed school and been successful there. They desire to expand their mental horizons, and some may have writing ability. They will most likely love getting out and travelling about, and much time and consideration will be given to the taking of short journeys. Relationships with siblings and neighbors are usually good.

JUPITER IN FOURTH HOUSE

Usually there's a happy and comfortable home life and good relationships with family members, and the family may be large. If aspects to Jupiter are good, the individual could prosper in the area of birth; if challenging, they may be better off settling somewhere far away. Most are of an upstanding nature, respected by the community. Fortunes may improve later in life.

JUPITER IN FIFTH HOUSE

They're creative in the arts, in sport, and/or in matters to do with children. They are fond of children, and their offspring are likely to do well, often gaining distinction at school. Some tend towards gambling or speculation; if aspects to Jupiter are challenging, this could turn out to be somewhat disastrous financially! Their love life is usually happy, and there may be an involvement with a person of means.

JUPITER IN SIXTH HOUSE

There's often an expansive and benevolent desire to work to help others, and when this is directed towards the field of medicine/healthcare, they can make extraordinarily good healers. As cheerful co-workers, they are liked and respected by colleagues. There should be no difficulty finding work, and it often pays very well. If there are difficult aspects to Jupiter, liver complaints may become a problem for those who indulge too heavily in rich food and drink.

JUPITER IN SEVENTH HOUSE

This can bring happy marriage, the individual being capable of giving selfless love, doing all they can to provide spiritual and material comfort for their partner. They may marry someone of wealth or status, and/or the marriage partner may be of another nationality or race. With challenging Jupiter aspects in this House, there can be disappointments due to expecting too much of the partner.

JUPITER IN EIGHTH HOUSE

A chance of gain through inheritance exists, although with challenging aspects there may be problems to do with there being legal difficulties or heavy taxation involved in this. Often there is talent for handling others' finances; work to do with accounting or insurance may be a good professional path to follow.

JUPITER IN NINTH HOUSE

There's love of serious subjects, study and travel. Talent for foreign languages is likely, and they may go to study abroad. Relationships with foreigners tend to be good, and they may have many foreign friends. Long-distance travel will be much enjoyed and may even be profitable. They're usually tolerant and open-minded with desire to learn about other cultures.

JUPITER IN TENTH HOUSE

Many are able to make a particularly successful and well-paid career. There may be quite a few opportunities, not least because their own ethical attitudes gain the respect of those higher up. Some may actually be *honest* politicians! Others can be good managers and business executives; some may have acting ability. Prominence may come in later life.

JUPITER IN ELEVENTH HOUSE

These people generally both have good friends and are good friends. They have extensive social circles and are well-liked. They're generous to their friends, and receive generosity in return. They may also get involved in organizations that help others. With challenging Jupiter aspects, however, some may incline towards sponging off friends instead!

JUPITER IN TWELFTH HOUSE

Many feel a need to expand themselves, psychologically or spiritually, and carry this out through solitary activities such as meditation, study, quiet reflection and the like. Imagination is strong and there's a lot of compassion and sympathy. Challenging aspects to Jupiter may bring impractical thinking that results in their ending up relying on the charity of others.

SATURN

SATURN IN FIRST HOUSE

Here we find those who seem to have a heavy 'karma', particularly if the aspects to Saturn are challenging. There can be huge responsibilities, limitations and hardships, especially in early life. Poor health is sometimes a problem. Some may be shy and inhibited in early years, needing a bit of a push to consciously cultivate a more outgoing attitude. There's deep psychological need to be recognized for one's own merits, and many with this position of Saturn work extra hard and accomplish much. Many have a slim, long-boned, classic 'Saturnine' appearance.

SATURN IN SECOND HOUSE

There's desire to acquire wealth and status, but it doesn't usually come easy – they find they have to work hard for these. There is a good chance of financial success but not without considerable struggle. Their attitude towards money is cautious, often due to a deep-seated fear of poverty. Challenging aspects to Saturn in this House may indicate much hard work for little financial gain.

SATURN IN THIRD HOUSE

In childhood, they take a serious view of school life. Some may have had their education limited in some way, or have found their school system too regimented. There's ability for practical thinking and mental discipline, and mathematical or scientific ability are likely. These people are cautious in speech and writing, careful about signing any sort of agreement or contract. There may have been responsibility for siblings in early life.

SATURN IN FOURTH HOUSE

There may be much responsibility to do with home and family. They might have had strict parents as a child. Some may find they have to assume financial responsibility for parents in later years. There's likely to be pride in family ancestry and a love of antiques and other old, traditional things.

SATURN IN FIFTH HOUSE

A cautious attitude is taken towards emotional relationships – some may seem stand-offish, but they are really only sizing up the situation. Often there is romantic involvement with an older or more mature sort of person. Some may have difficult children, or above-average responsibility concerning them. Musical talent, especially for complicated works, is possible.

SATURN IN SIXTH HOUSE

Much capacity for efficiency here – work is taken seriously and with pride, and may entail a fair amount of responsibility. With good aspects to Saturn, these people are liked and respected by co-workers and employers; if aspects are challenging, there may be disharmony in the work environment due to the person being thought of as a bit of a 'wet blanket'. Challenging aspects may also give health problems due to low vitality.

SATURN IN SEVENTH HOUSE

They may marry late in life, and/or the partner may be considerably older or more serious. There's a good sense of responsibility towards marriage and other partnerships. Good aspects to Saturn in this House may bestow a lasting, stable marriage, while challenging ones could indicate restrictions or limitations of some kind. There is ability to work well in co-operation with others.

SATURN IN EIGHTH HOUSE

They may be responsible for the financial affairs of others, possibly in looking after their partner's taxes, insurance and so on, or through work concerning the management of other people's money. In any case, this individual's attitude in these matters is cautious and careful. There may be studious interest in the subjects of the occult and the afterlife, and this position of Saturn usually brings longevity so there's plenty of time to ponder on those subjects!

SATURN IN NINTH HOUSE

This is often the mark of the deep thinker. Concentration tends to be good, and there's usually serious desire to pursue higher education and achieve distinction for it. Long-distance travel may be undertaken for business purposes and dealings with older foreigners might be of benefit. With challenging aspects to Saturn, some may be a little on the intolerant, self-righteous side.

SATURN IN TENTH HOUSE

Real 'career man/career woman' types appear here: ambitions are extra strong and there's all-consuming desire for fame, status and financial reward. They are willing to work hard to achieve success; which is a good thing because often (with challenging Saturn aspects, especially) there are obstacles and disappointments along the way. Many become respected authorities in their field.

SATURN IN ELEVENTH HOUSE

A serious and responsible attitude is taken towards friends and social activities. Often they have friends who are of help in their career, and many of their friends may be of a much older age group, and/or of a more notably 'mature' outlook than average for their ages. Loyalty and fairness towards friends are strong traits.

SATURN IN TWELFTH HOUSE

Many of these people like to spend a lot of time in seclusion. They tend to be secretive and to hide their sorrows from others. There can be an inclination towards depression, especially if there are challenging Saturn aspects. Work may be carried out 'behind the scenes', possibly concerned with medicine or psychology, and there's ability to sacrifice self for the good of those less fortunate.

URANUS

URANUS IN FIRST HOUSE

They like to be unconventional and free in self-expression, sometimes to the point of being considered pretty eccentric! Originality and ingenuity are to the fore, and there can be considerable scientific talent, even genius. They are seekers of the unusual, liking change and lots of excitement in their lives. Security tends to be of not much importance to them. Often those with Uranus here are of striking appearance, and they can be unusually tall.

URANUS IN SECOND HOUSE

An erratic financial situation is often their fate: money comes, and equally goes, suddenly or unexpectedly. There have talent for making money from original and/or unusual sources. They're especially likely to profit from electronics, computers, or some other high-tech scientific field.

URANUS IN THIRD HOUSE

Many original thinkers have Uranus here; their minds are open to new experiences and not swayed by outmoded manners of thinking. They will usually have had a flair for maths and sciences in school. New angles on things may come through flashes of sudden inspiration. Short journeys may be taken on impulse.

URANUS IN FOURTH HOUSE

Their home life is probably unusual in some manner. Ultramodern decor is popular, plus a liking for electronic gadgets. One of their parents may be extraordinary in some way. There may be sudden changes of residence.

URANUS IN FIFTH HOUSE

Love life can be changeable; relationships may come about and/or end unexpectedly. They're attracted to those who are 'different', unconventional, original. In creative matters, there's ability for much originality, for being ahead of one's time.

URANUS IN SIXTH HOUSE

They are able to come up with original and advanced ideas in their line of work. They may formulate inventions or make worthwhile discoveries. Some are attracted to careers to do with alternative medicine, or if of a more orthodox medical outlook, they may take an interest in experimental or hypothetical methods of treatment.

URANUS IN SEVENTH HOUSE

Often, the marriage conditions and/or partner are unusual in some way, and they are attracted to partners who are original in thought and somewhat unconventional. Marriage may occur or end suddenly and unexpectedly. They feel a need to retain a good deal of freedom within their relationships; many relationships may tend to be short-lived.

URANUS IN EIGHTH HOUSE

Sudden changes in finances, either for good or for bad, can be common with Uranus here. There could be unexpected situations to do with other people's money. For some, there's possibility of an unexpected inheritance. Some have a particularly keen interest in the mysteries of life, and may formulate their own advanced and original ideas about that sphere of things.

URANUS IN NINTH HOUSE

Strange events might occur while engaged in long distance travel. Long journeys may be taken on sudden impulse, and they enjoy travel as a means of excitement and stimulation. Ideas on religion, education and philosophical subjects are likely to be far-sighted and advanced.

URANUS IN TENTH HOUSE

Unusual professions and hatred of conventional work are common with these individuals. There's intense dislike of being in a subordinate position in their place of work – this person likes to left alone to get on with doing their job their own way, and really detests constant supervision. There may be many changes in career, due in part to their low boredom threshold, and in part to their employer's difficulty in understanding these Uranian types. There may be sudden rises to fame (and sudden drops as well!).

URANUS IN ELEVENTH HOUSE

They like to have unconventional friends who will provide mental stimulation and new ideas. They may make friends quickly and lose friends equally suddenly. There's often a tolerant outlook and a wish to help in bettering existing social conditions, though they prefer to give this assistance in an impersonal, detached sort of way, not getting emotionally involved with those they aid.

URANUS IN TWELFTH HOUSE

There's strong attraction towards the unusual, which many of these people may feel they have to keep hidden for fear of ridicule. They are prone to sudden flashes of insight from the subconscious, and are highly intuitive.

NEPTUNE

NEPTUNE IN FIRST HOUSE

They are highly imaginative, intuitive, sensitive and idealistic, sometimes seemingly psychic. There can be artistic or musical ability, which may seem as if inspired from another world; indeed there can be a quality of unworldliness about these people in general. They may have an almost ethereal appearance, the eyes possessing a dreamy or magnetic look. Under challenging aspects to Neptune, they may need to guard against attraction towards overdoing the alcohol or drugs or other negative forms of escapism.

NEPTUNE IN SECOND HOUSE

There's an idealistic attitude towards finances and the use of them. They may dream up imaginative ways of making money, but money may also disappear through mysterious circumstances (or, by their simply being a spendthrift!). Some may be impractical about money and can be subject to being taken advantage of financially.

NEPTUNE IN THIRD HOUSE

There's a specially imaginative mind, though in matters to do with the intellect there can be lack of concentration and a tendency to digress through stream-of-consciousness thinking. They like to dream. There may be difficulties with misunderstandings over contracts, agreements and so on. Short trips by water are liked.

NEPTUNE IN FOURTH HOUSE

High ideals about home and family combine with an emotional bond to these. One of the parents may be somewhat mysterious: maybe someone who disappears from time to time, or maybe an alcoholic or similar. There may be family secrets, 'skeletons in the cupboard'. They often specially enjoy living by the sea or other body of water.

NEPTUNE IN FIFTH HOUSE

Imaginative and intuitive ability can be applied to the arts, especially the performing arts. Artistic ability is probable, and there's talent for acting or dancing. They're romantic and consider love relationships to be of utmost importance, but, there can be mysterious or secretive circumstances surrounding some of these affairs.

NEPTUNE IN SIXTH HOUSE

They are imaginative in their work, but difficulties in

concentration and applying themselves may impede progress. Some may be attracted towards spiritual types of work, such as spiritual healing. Some find that they have sensitivity towards drugs, medicines, alcohol or certain foods, or have unusual allergies.

NEPTUNE IN SEVENTH HOUSE

The marriage partner will often be of an artistic and/or mystical type. In some cases, there's a sort of telepathic link between the partners, maybe with each of them often finishing what the other began to say. With challenging aspects, there could be an element of misunderstanding within the marriage.

NEPTUNE IN EIGHTH HOUSE

There may be some area of confusion regarding financial issues such as taxes or insurance. There's sometimes interest in occult matters and if there are good aspects to Neptune there may be some psychic ability. With challenging aspects, there's a need to be wary against overdosing on medications or alcohol as these people can be extra sensitive to those things.

NEPTUNE IN NINTH HOUSE

Idealism regarding spiritual, philosophical or educational values is evident. With some, there may be attraction to mysticism. Often there's love of long-distance travel, especially by sea. Some spiritually-orientated individuals may make religious pilgrimages.

NEPTUNE IN TENTH HOUSE

Intuitive abilities may help to further this individual's career. Their profession is likely to be unusual or to require a good deal of intuition. The career may involve religious work, psychology or other work that involves helping others, or maybe something to do with the sea. There may be several changes in the direction of the career.

NEPTUNE IN ELEVENTH HOUSE

Their friends tend to be of an idealistic, imaginative type. There may be a strong telepathic link with their closest friends, many of whom will be of a specially kind and helpful sort. These people may join societies that are based on spiritual principles or that are to do with the psychic sciences. With challenging aspects, some friends may be turn out to be deceitful or unreliable.

NEPTUNE IN TWELFTH HOUSE

Imagination and intuition are high and this individual is ultra-sensitive. Many are able to tune into their subconscious, and some may have psychic ability. They need lots of time on their own, to take refuge and recharge their batteries. Artistic talent is possible, often for acting or dancing.

PLUTO

PLUTO IN FIRST HOUSE

This makes for an intense, dynamic individual, with much willpower and determination. They're likely to have a piercing gaze and an aura of magnetism and energy. There is often desire to improve themselves and their surroundings, to transform and regenerate. Their lives may be subject to different phases not of their own choosing, but they are generally able to cope with these changes well.

PLUTO IN SECOND HOUSE

There may be a sort of 'back and forth' effect on their financial situation; sometimes well-off, sometimes dire straits. There is capacity for finding previously hidden ways of making money, and many can gain lucrative income by regenerating a previously failing business or by having more than one source of income.

PLUTO IN THIRD HOUSE

These people are outspoken and like to express their opinions forcefully. They're stubborn in their beliefs and not well-disposed towards changing them, even in light of hard evidence! The mind is keen and penetrating, and they are eager to get to the bottom of things.

PLUTO IN FOURTH HOUSE

They like to work to improve their home environment. Feelings for family members are intense, whether for better or worse – some may be domineering in the home environment. There's often something out-of-the-ordinary about the family background or one of their parents.

PLUTO IN FIFTH HOUSE

Dynamic creative power is found here. Much intensity is put into self expression and into love affairs, of which there are likely to be many. Some may take a sensationalistic view of their love lives!

PLUTO IN SIXTH HOUSE

Many have a strong drive to reform and improve work conditions. They are hard workers and will drive themselves to breaking point to achieve recognition. Some may suffer health problems caused by a blockage of some sort (many sufferers of constipation are found here, oh dear) and may have to make corrections in their diet. Interest in health is common.

PLUTO IN SEVENTH HOUSE

There may be some type of unusual, coming-and-going circumstances to do with marriage or other long-term relationship: maybe a stormy, on again off again relationship, or a partner who disappears from time to time. They tend to choose a partner of a magnetic, dynamic type and maybe also a little domineering. Or, conversely, they may themselves be dominant towards their partner. There's good business ability and much work of importance can be accomplished with a partner.

PLUTO IN EIGHTH HOUSE

They may be of the type that takes life very seriously - a real 'do or die' attitude. They're intense and passionate about everything. There is often interest in unsolved crimes, life after death, and other mysteries.

PLUTO IN NINTH HOUSE

A marked desire to learn and experience everything possible. Knowledge is eagerly digested by these people in order to transform themselves through intellectual growth. Sometimes there is a wish to reform and regenerate the social order.

PLUTO IN TENTH HOUSE

Great will to succeed in the career is usually evident. They'll fight their way to the top and want to be recognized as leaders in their field. Most are good at assuming positions of power, but some with challenging aspects may incline towards being tyrannical.

PLUTO IN ELEVENTH HOUSE

They are often loners, but those friends they do have tend to be enduring, loyal pals many of whom may be interested in social reform or in crime, or in mysteries in general. This individual may join groups to do with these subjects. Friendships tend to come and go throughout the person's life.

PLUTO IN TWELFTH HOUSE

These people are able to get in tune with their subconscious minds and gain much insight. There's likely to be considerable (though possibly secret) interest in mysterious things and the inner workings of the mind. They can be very secretive and from time to time feel a need for total seclusion.

THE ASPECTS

THE SUN

SUN-MOON

The conjunction may make the person somewhat one-sided; their ego is strongly wrapped up in their emotions.

If aspects between the Sun and Moon are challenging, they may show conflict within the personality. Sometimes, with difficult aspects, there's just a general feeling of dissatisfaction and lack of fulfillment.

With good aspects between these two, there is harmony between the conscious and the subconscious, the selfhood and the emotions. These individuals are often of a calm, well-balanced disposition.

SUN-MERCURY

As the Sun and Mercury are never more than 28º apart, the only aspect they can make is the conjunction, which gives forceful and creative thinking in those who have it. Stubbornness is also a frequently-found trait.

SUN-VENUS

These two planets are never more than 48º apart, and so a conjunction is the only aspect they can make. This indicates strong and vigorous emotions, this person being able to give affection freely and to bring happiness to others. They have charm and are attractive and eager to be liked. Some may have artistic or musical talent.

SUN-MARS

The conjunction gives hardworking ability coupled with strength and courage. The sign and House in which the conjunction is found will indicate the area of life in which these abilities can be directed. Over-enthusiasm can lead to accident-proneness.

Good Sun-Mars aspects bestow willpower, health and physical strength. These people can work at a high energy level for amazingly long periods.

Challenging aspects denote impatience, impulsiveness and a tendency to jump to conclusions. There may be a liking for hazard and risk-taking – an adrenaline junkie.

SUN-JUPITER

The conjunction and good Sun-Jupiter aspects are very fortunate to have, bringing good luck and success not least as a result of their own generous and beneficent nature. Their outlook is positive and cheerful, and they just about always possess a good sense of humor.

Challenging aspects may indicate extravagance of a badly-judged and wasteful type. They can be restless, reckless and careless. Too much of a liking for drink and rich food may bring health problems and overweight.

SUN-SATURN

The conjunction and good aspects bring hardworking ability and ambition, with (especially in the conjunction) strong drive to achieve goals of the highest standard. Powers of concentration are usually good and they can be patient and self-disciplined.

Challenging aspects can bring obstacles along the path to success, with much effort needed to overcome them. But many of these people, spurred on by the extra challenge, are able to go on to accomplish things that those with an easier life find too daunting.

SUN-URANUS

Those with the conjunction and good aspects are unpredictable, original, maybe a little odd, and often totally fascinating. Inventiveness and vision can be found, with talent for maths, computers and the sciences. There may be lack of tact, but enthusiasm, humor and sparkle make up for it.

Challenging aspects can bring nervous tension and rash behavior. With Sun square Uranus in particular, they may knock down what they've taken a long time to build and ignore good advice from others – 'shooting themselves in the foot' is an apt phrase here! Like the good aspects, there's much originality, but in this case there can be difficulty in giving it concrete form.

SUN-NEPTUNE

The conjunction and good aspects give imagination and intuition which are put to use in creative expression. Many are talented in the arts and their work may appear to have come from some sort of otherworldly inspiration. There may be a spiritual, ethereal quality to this person. There's sensitivity to the suffering of others and a high emotional level.

Challenging aspects sometimes indicate lack of self-confidence, possibly leaving themselves vulnerable to being taken advantage of by unscrupulous types. Some may, themselves, have manipulative tendencies.

SUN-PLUTO

The conjunction and good aspects give excellent recuperative powers and an ability for regenerating and transforming all areas of life. They have a powerful and forceful manner of expression. With the conjunction, much intensity and passion are directed towards the area signified by the sign and House occupied.

Challenging aspects can bring domineering and over-forceful tendencies. There may be an inclination towards wanting to force one's own views upon others.

SUN-ASCENDANT

The conjunction doubly emphasizes the qualities of the Sun sign, for better or for worse!

Good aspects help give energy and enthusiasm, with blending of inner thoughts and outward expression. The more positive traits of the two signs concerned are emphasized.

Challenging aspects may bring a conflict between what they feel themselves to be deep down, and what they present on the surface.

SUN-MIDHEAVEN

Conjunction and good aspects indicate that their identity and personality are strongly tied up with their career. There's leadership ability and the capacity for being of considerable influence through the profession.

Challenging aspects may bring conflict with employers, parents or other authority figures. Obstacles along the way may force this person to work specially hard for success.

THE MOON

MOON-MERCURY

The conjunction indicates that their thinking is strongly influenced by their own emotions or by appeals to their emotions. Thought and speech show imaginativeness, and there may be a whimsical streak.

Good aspects often denote a good memory and common sense. They also help strengthen the health and keep nervous tension to a minimum.

Challenging aspects can give a nervous disposition and some may allow their emotions to interfere too much with their judgment. Hypersensitivity is likely.

MOON-VENUS

The conjunction and good aspects tend to bring charm, sensitivity and tact. These people are sociable and popular, and good at putting others at ease. There's usually love of art, music, comfort and beauty. Some have an artistic appearance.

Challenging aspects may bring disappointments in emotional relationships; sometimes inability to express feelings is to blame. Some may hide a shy or moody nature by trying to put up an aggressive exterior.

MOON-MARS

The conjunction brings very strong feelings – whether for better or worse will depend on the rest of the chart! Conjunction and good aspects give good health and lots of energy. They are honest and genuine, and willing to fight for their beliefs.

Challenging aspects may bring stormy emotions, a tendency to become easily upset. Some can be of an irritable nature and provoke quarrels and be prone to angry outbursts. Independence and willfulness are strong.

MOON-JUPITER

The conjunction and good aspects indicate a generous and benevolent nature, protective and willing to help others. There's fondness for comfort and luxury (maybe overly so with the conjunction). For some, long distance travel or a period of living abroad may be of great benefit.

Challenging aspects may bring extravagance and/or over-emotionalism, and some may be so prone to self-indulgence that health suffers as a result. There may be inner conflicts over religion or some lack of judgment in emotional matters.

MOON-SATURN

The conjunction and good aspects help stabilize the emotions, bringing caution and practicality in that sphere of things. They spend some time sizing other people up before letting them get close. Powers of endurance are strong and they are able to be self-sacrificing in the line of duty.

Challenging aspects may be indicative of a melancholy type of person, the proverbial 'wet blanket'. They might need to make a conscious effort to cultivate humor and a more positive, cheerful outlook.

MOON-URANUS

The conjunction often gives a strong emotional need to be considered 'different'. Sudden changes of mood may make them seem erratic and downright peculiar to others. Good aspects and the conjunction all bestow an exciting, sparkly nature that fascinates other people. There's always a craving for new and exciting experiences.

Challenging aspects bring restlessness and irritability; and there can also be disruptions in the home life. Much inventiveness is shown but there can sometimes be a perverse inclination to throw away the results of one's labors.

MOON-NEPTUNE

Conjunction and good aspects give vivid imagination which can be put to good use in art, music, writing and acting. They are impressionable and very receptive to the moods of others, willing to lend a sympathetic ear and to help if they can. They enjoy daydreaming and can have particularly vivid dreams.

Challenging aspects may bring muddle in things to do with the emotions. Care needs to be taken not to wallow in negative emotions but to find a more positive outlet for them.

MOON-PLUTO

The conjunction and good aspects give intense emotions. These are easier to control with the good aspects than with the conjunction. There is fearlessness, and obstacles are taken on with courage and persistence. Recuperative abilities are usually excellent.

Challenging aspects may bring explosive changes of mood, impatience and jealousy. They may be ruled by a compulsion to destroy the past, and/or may want to force changes within their domestic situation.

MOON-ASCENDANT

Conjunction and good aspects bring good memory and ability to express emotions positively. If the Moon is in the first House, the face is usually round and full, and there may be a tendency to overweight.

Challenging aspects may give difficulty in expressing emotions and making decisions. These individuals are sensitive and can be emotionally vulnerable.

MOON-MIDHEAVEN

Conjunction and good aspects can bring popularity in the work environment and the possibility of coming before the public eye. They're often able to advance in the career through being emotionally in tune with the needs of their bosses and/or their customers.

Challenging aspects may signify difficulties in the career. Work conditions may be changeable, this person never knowing quite where they stand.

MERCURY

MERCURY-VENUS

The conjunction and the sextile (the only major aspects these two can make as they are never more than 76º apart) bestow grace and skill in speech and writing. There may be talent for music, especially singing-songwriting. Any pastime that involves the expression of beauty is likely to appeal. Many have pleasant-sounding voices.

MERCURY-MARS

The conjunction and good aspects give lively minds. Mental energy and assertiveness in speech and writing are likely, and there may be ability to apply oneself to long-term study (although restlessness may be problematic). Usually there's fondness for fast walking and fast driving.

Challenging aspects give a mind that is active and energetic but that may be easily roused to anger and argumentativeness. There may be nervous tension and an irritable streak. Headaches are common.

MERCURY-JUPITER

Conjunction and good aspects usually give desire to expand the mental faculties and to learn as much as possible. Studying is enjoyed, and these people like to have well-stocked home libraries. Broad-mindedness is usually a strong trait.

Challenging aspects may give an impractical tendency to think up grand schemes that are too extravagant or unrealistic to be carried out. Some may tend to promise more than they can deliver.

MERCURY-SATURN

The conjunction and good aspects are indicative of logical, exacting thinking, mental organization, and scientific or mathematical flair. Concentration is usually very good. They can be patient and apply themselves to precise, methodical types of work.

Challenging aspects may give a blunt attitude, harshness

and abruptness in speech. There can be a tendency to place too much importance on rules and regulations. Some may like to plot and scheme.

MERCURY-URANUS

The conjunction and good aspects give originality in thought and a mind that works with the speed of lightning. There can be inclination towards scientific subjects, and brilliance may be in evidence.

Challenging aspects give originality (or what some may consider eccentricity) of thought and a quick mind, but these attributes may not always be used wisely. Some may be prone to 'harebrained schemes', and mental energy may be wasted.

MERCURY-NEPTUNE

Conjunction and good aspects give vivid imagination and insightful awareness of the workings of the subconscious mind. They can be artists, writers and composers, and some may have telepathic ability. They're usually of a gentle disposition and they dislike harshness and disharmony.

Challenging aspects may give absent-mindedness and misunderstandings. Imagination and intuition are strong but may not always be used to good purpose: the fertile imagination may itself invent things to worry about!

MERCURY-PLUTO

Those with the conjunction or good aspects have

mentalities of a penetrating, persistent nature; they like to get to the bottom of things, to understand why things are the way they are. Life's mysteries hold great fascination. They may enjoy crime novels or TV detective shows and being an amateur sleuth, or may work in that field of things..

Challenging aspects may give bluntness of speech and lack of regard for others' feelings. They can be secretive and some may indulge in plotting and scheming in private. Nervous tension may be a problem for them.

MERCURY-ASCENDANT

The conjunction and good aspects give mental energy and ability. They're talkative and they enjoy reading, writing and getting out a lot. With the conjunction, restlessness may be strong and they may have a highly-strung nature and appearance.

Challenging aspects could signify a difficulty in communicating or in getting out and about. This may be due to an actual physical cause, or there may generally be misunderstandings with others at times. They can be prone to nervous tension and, again, restlessness.

MERCURY-MIDHEAVEN

Good aspects and conjunction may bring success in the career through ability to communicate well with both employers and the public. The sort of work preferred will usually be of a mental rather than manual type. With the conjunction, some may become bored easily and change jobs frequently.

Challenging aspects may bring difficulties in the career

due to lack of communication. Some may find lack of higher education to be a stumbling block in the pursuit of their career.

VENUS

VENUS-MARS

The conjunction and good aspects signify emotional vitality. This quality may be expressed through artistic creativity, or simply through overindulgence in their love life! There is just about always a zest for life, and they're usually specially attractive to the opposite sex.

Challenging aspects may indicate problems in the love life and in emotional life in general; a quarrelsome attitude may be taken towards their loved ones. Men may display coarse behavior, and women may be annoyingly temperamental.

VENUS-JUPITER

Conjunction and good aspects make for someone who is a charmer in a big way, oozing with generosity and warmth, which makes them well liked. They like to entertain, to play the good host. There's sympathy for the unfortunate and desire to help. There is often a sense of joy in life and the ability to spread this feeling to others.

Challenging aspects may incline some towards laziness and self-indulgence. Emotions run to extremes and some may exaggerate things. A craving for luxury and an overly flowery sentimentalism may be apparent.

VENUS-SATURN

The conjunction and good aspects bring a sense of responsibility and fair play in emotional relationships. There's great capacity for loyalty to the loved one and close friends. Sometimes there will be a large age difference between the person and their romantic partners.

Challenging aspects may give difficulty in expressing feelings and they may be snide about the partner's faults. There can be some bad luck in relationships, sometimes due to picking the wrong types of partner.

VENUS-URANUS

The conjunction and good aspects can signify sudden, unexpected love affairs (which may end just as suddenly). With the conjunction, a strong emotional need for excitement may make the person seem quite a wild sort of a guy or gal! They are fun-loving types who are always full of surprises. Some may have artistic talent of an especially distinctive sort.

Challenging aspects may show a willful need to be considered emotionally unconventional, and unusual relationships tend to be sought. More than a few broken relationships are likely.

VENUS-NEPTUNE

Good aspects and conjunction indicate a highly sensitive

type, often romantic and unworldly. There can be artistic talent of a specially ethereal sort and a love of soft, soothing music. Kindness and empathy are strong traits and they are always willing to help.

Challenging aspects may bring disillusionment in emotional relationships; the other party may not be as nice or reliable as this person thinks they are. Some may have to be secretive about their love affairs.

VENUS-PLUTO

All aspects: There is often a feeling that the relationships of these people are somehow fated: there can be love at first sight which in these cases actually turns out to be much more than just a physical attraction. They love ardently and totally, some feeling 'reborn' through their relationship.

Challenging aspects can signify that a number of the person's relationships may be disrupted due to circumstances beyond their control.

VENUS-ASCENDANT

The conjunction and good aspects generally bring personal beauty and charm. These people are graceful, pleasant and sociable and therefore easily liked. Many are very fortunate in general, and as a result some may become a bit spoiled!

Challenging aspects may indicate some difficulty expressing feelings. They may be hypersensitive, and some may express themselves in a coarse manner.

VENUS-MIDHEAVEN

Conjunction and good aspects often bring success in the career. They are able to advance through the positive use of charm and grace. An artistic career may be followed.

Challenging aspects may signify emotional dissatisfaction with the career. Sometimes their love life (if Venus is in the fifth House) or home life (if Venus is in the fourth House) interferes with efficiency at the job.

MARS

MARS-JUPITER

With the conjunction, these people pour loads of energy and enthusiasm into the area signified by the sign and House position of the conjunction. Good aspects add a positive outlook on life plus often a love of travel. They're active and enjoy sport and physical exercise, and are also willing to fight for what's right.

Challenging aspects can bring restlessness and recklessness. These individuals want constant stimulation and find it very hard to relax. Some may be militant types, believing in fighting for causes that may not be all that worthy.

MARS-SATURN

The conjunction can be problematic: the urge for action signified by Mars conflicts with the inhibiting and restricting qualities of Saturn. Good aspects are easier to get on with – they give ability for well-considered, practical action. These people don't waste any energy and use all their resources for maximum effect.

Challenging aspects bring uneven energy flow; sometimes they feel very energetic, at others they feel gripped by total inertia. Enthusiasm wears off quickly.

MARS-URANUS

With the conjunction we find people with a strong sense of rebelliousness. They may be of the 'revolutionary' type. Both the conjunction and the good aspects give an individual with a craving for continual excitement and who possesses lots of physical energy.

Challenging aspects may incline towards unwise impulsive actions. The craving for excitement may conflict with practicality. A quarrelsome streak is possible, and the temper can be frighteningly explosive.

MARS-NEPTUNE

The conjunction and good aspects bring imagination and often active interest in spiritual or psychic matters. If there are artistic abilities, the work they turn out will be of a vibrant type with a romantic edge.

Challenging aspects may indicate negative escapism, and some may be overly-sensitive to medicines or allergens. Some may incline towards secretive deceitful actions. There is sometimes low physical vitality.

MARS-PLUTO

The conjunction and good aspects indicate high levels of endurance, recuperative abilities and stamina. There is ability to make new beginnings comfortably and to cope with drastic change.

Challenging aspects give courage and energy, but these may sometimes be applied to less than constructive purposes, which may be pursued doggedly despite having been proved impractical. They may also frighten or overwhelm others with an overly forceful nature!

MARS-ASCENDANT

The conjunction and good aspects indicate someone active and energetic, often with a well-above-average physical constitution, great endurance and ridiculous reserves of energy. Assertiveness and competitiveness are strong traits, and they probably enjoy competitive games and sports.

Challenging aspects may signify an overly aggressive nature that can put other people off. If Mars is in the tenth House there may be trouble getting on with employers, or an over-zealousness for promotion that annoys colleagues!

MARS-MIDHEAVEN

The conjunction and easy aspects show that these people can put loads of energy into the profession and that they are generally very ambitious. They want to be well-known and to be considered important. They will fight hard get to the top.

Challenging aspects may indicate difficulty getting along with those in positions of authority. A need to control impatience and headstrongness is very much needed if they want to achieve success.

JUPITER

JUPITER-SATURN

Good aspects and conjunction can give excellent ability to achieve much through hard work and careful planning. They are able to apply patience and self-discipline to build things, or to create conditions, that are of real and lasting value.

Challenging aspects may bring disappointments in achieving goals, sometimes through inability to be aware of their own limitations. There may be difficulty taking advantage of opportunities that arise, either through lack of self-confidence or just plain bad luck.

JUPITER-URANUS

Conjunction and good aspects bring ability to make

progress in life through unexpected or unusual gains or opportunities.

Challenging aspects can indicate restlessness and a tendency to go too far in the search for constant excitement and adventure. They may get involved in impractical schemes.

JUPITER-NEPTUNE

Those with the conjunction and good aspects have the potential for a vivid and prolific imagination. There is usually affection for animals.

Challenging aspects show that they are capable of much kindness and sympathy but may be impractical about the way they show it: they may give unselfish help to those who don't actually deserve or appreciate the effort.

JUPITER-PLUTO

Those with the conjunction and good aspects are usually very capable at making new beginnings and at building on the foundations of things that have previously been destroyed.

Challenging aspects may bring a not overly helpful rebellious streak. The person may want to overthrow existing conditions just for the sake of it, without actually having improved anything in the process.

JUPITER-ASCENDANT

Good aspects and conjunction bring a cheerful, self-confident, benevolent streak. The disposition is enthusiastic and expansive. If Jupiter is in the first House, they will usually have a large build.

Challenging aspects may incline them to exaggerate and to get easily carried away. Some could also come across as uncomfortably overwhelming and bombastic!

JUPITER-MIDHEAVEN

Those with the conjunction and good aspects may be remarkably successful in their careers, some even being an example of a rags-to-riches scenario.

Challenging aspects sometimes warn that an inflated ego may stand in the way of career progress. Some may behave in an exaggerated, over-the-top manner.

SATURN, URANUS, NEPTUNE, AND PLUTO

As the slow-moving planets stay in the same sign for years, their aspects to each other have a large-scale, generational effect rather than a specific individual one, and we won't cover those in this small book. However, the aspects they make to the Ascendant and the Midheaven will affect the individual specifically, so we will give a rundown of those here:

SATURN-ASCENDANT

Conjunction and good aspects add practicality and common sense, reliability and trustworthiness. The conjunction may add a tendency to depression, and can often give a lanky appearance.

Challenging aspects can bring difficulty in displaying friendliness openly, giving the person an aloof manner.

SATURN-MIDHEAVEN

The conjunction and the good aspects often indicate someone who is willing to work hard for career advancement, applying careful planning.

Challenging aspects may bring obstacles in the path to success, though these may spur them to work harder and ultimately achieve more.

URANUS-ASCENDANT

The conjunction usually gives an unusual appearance, often a very tall stature. Good aspects bring originality and inventiveness, with a distinctive method of self-expression.

Challenging aspects can bring nervous tension and a tendency to erratic behavior.

URANUS-MIDHEAVEN

Conjunction/good aspects often bring an unusual career and/or the ability to come up with new, inventive ideas regarding their work. They may work in computers or another modern high-tech field.

Challenging aspects indicate difficulty in conforming to the rules of the workplace and a tendency to change jobs frequently.

NEPTUNE-ASCENDANT

The conjunction can give an other-worldly appearance and manner, plus imagination and artistry. They like to dream and to escape. Good aspects indicate that their well-developed imagination and intuitive instincts can be put to good use, and there may be telepathic ability.

Challenging aspects may bring misunderstanding in social relationships due to being 'in a world of their own' much of the time. Some may be prone to inner conflicts over religion or the spiritual side of life. An inclination towards negative escapism may need to be overcome.

NEPTUNE-MIDHEAVEN

Good aspects and conjunction show much use of the imagination in their career. Their profession may be unusual, and may have to do with the arts, the sea, or helping others.

Challenging aspects can indicate confusion over their career. Some may be dissatisfied with their job and spend a lot of the workday daydreaming (a Walter Mitty type, maybe!). Some may find it hard to be reliable, or may have unreliable employers.

PLUTO-ASCENDANT

Conjunction and good aspects often indicate someone of an intense, dynamic sort who can have a charismatic effect on others. They have an urge to reform, to remake their situations into something more beneficial for both themselves and others.

Challenging aspects may signify an anti-social, secretive streak. Some may want to remake others who don't want to be remade, to force their own ideas on unwilling subjects. Nervous tension may be a problem.

PLUTO-MIDHEAVEN

The conjunction and good aspects show someone who likes to continually remake and better their career, always looking for something new to build on old foundations. They are able to make drastic changes in their careers in order to follow something that will be of greater benefit in the long run.

Challenging aspects may bring difficulty at work, due to their attempts at reforming their work conditions not going down well with their employer!

AND FINALLY:

SUGGESTIONS FOR FURTHER LEARNING

Well, that's it. If you've stuck with me for this long and if I've explained stuff clearly enough, you now know enough to draw up and interpret a basic birth chart.

I strongly recommend that you read other astrology books in addition to this one, both for beginners and for more advanced astrologers, in order to glean the maximum amount of knowledge and to get examples of how different astrologers create and interpret charts, as we will all have our own individual styles and ideas. Then you can put it all together and develop your own unique individual style.

Going on from here, there are many other areas of astrology you may like to find out more about. This book only intends to teach you the very basics and therefore save you from 'information overload' to begin with. But you may want to go on to explore more advanced subjects such as:

- House systems other than Equal House

- Use of secondary interpretational items such as the Moon's Nodes, the Part of Fortune, the fixed stars, the asteroids, and the weaker aspects

- Progressions and transits (astrological forecasting)

- Synastry (comparison of two charts for compatibility)

- Hindu astrology, Chinese astrology

- Relocation astrology (determining parts of the world where a person may be happiest)

- Rectifying (a way of devising a hypothetical estimated birth time for those whose time of birth is unknown)

Thank you for reading this book, and best wishes in your astrological journey!

ABOUT THE AUTHOR

Esme Morgan (pen name) practiced professional astrology in the
west London area for over twenty years. Now 'retired' from
astrological practice, she currently pursues writing as a career and
hopes this book will help new aspiring astrologers learn to do
charts.

Made in the USA
Coppell, TX
13 April 2022